CONGRESSIONAL
ELECTIONS
1896-1944

◇◇◇

CONGRESSIONAL ELECTIONS
1896-1944

The Sectional Basis of Political Democracy
in the House of Representatives

BY CORTEZ A. M. EWING

NORMAN : UNIVERSITY OF OKLAHOMA PRESS : 1947

◇◇◇

136082

BY CORTEZ A. M. EWING

Judges of the Supreme Court, 1789–1937
(MINNEAPOLIS, 1938)

*Presidential Elections: from Abraham Lincoln
to Franklin D. Roosevelt*
(NORMAN, 1940)

Congressional Elections, 1896–1944
(NORMAN, 1947)

To My Friend

THE HONORABLE A. S. (MIKE) MONRONEY
Member of Congress, Fifth District of Oklahoma, who has done
more than his share to infuse into the Congress the spirit of a
great parliamentary institution,
*this study is respectfully
dedicated*

◇◇◇

Preface

THE spectacular development of the economic order shoul-
dered many responsibilities upon the Congress of the United
States. Demands were heard from every quarter for the Congress, as the central organ of direction, to provide more and
better means for the good life. Opposed were certain persons
with proper feelings of nostalgia for the good old days of work
and frugality and organization of advantage. All over the world
parliamentary bodies were asked to provide procedures by
which the fortunes of specific groups would be enhanced; and
as those groups multiplied in number, the legislative halls became essentially diplomatic meeting-places for the achievement
of compromises among conflicting economic aspirations. Gone
were the days when parliaments sought to formulate the general
laws of eternal truth, as the natural-law theorists were wont to
remark in their enthusiasm for the ultimate unfolding of the
perfectly articulated society.

Fears for the future of middle-class society have, I suppose,
persisted since the years of Adam Smith and, later, of the utili-
tarians. But with the formation of industrial trusts, the pall of
pessimism increased in intellectual circles. During the Artificial
Decade, when Presidents Harding, Coolidge, and Hoover pre-
sided over the destinies of our country, popular esteem for the
Congress suffered a steady diminution. Party labels came to
represent little more than proper identification in the electoral
processes. Once in the halls of the Congress, the party label became meaningless.

My interest in the political basis of the Congress arose in
those years when that fundamental institution surrendered to

sheer opportunism and became, in the words of a few deprecatory critics, a mere "rubber stamp" for the New Deal executive department. Emergency stopgaps and even long-range political blueprints were almost exclusively the products of groups gathered about the President and his powerful administrative assistants.

Collection of the constituency election returns was started in 1938. Originally it was intended to gather all Congressional voting statistics from the Civil War to the present, but the difficulty of finding official figures for the individual contests for the eighties and before forced the decision to confine the investigation to the period starting in 1896. Under ordinary conditions the study would have been concluded by early 1942; but the critical condition of the world after 1939 did little to produce an atmosphere in which serious scholarship could be completed.

Wars, especially the total wars of the modern scene, take from scholars the will to pursue research problems which are not directly related to collective triumph. One may understand the transcendent genius of a Hegel, who was provoked to display his irritation at the noise produced by Napoleon's legions marching beneath his study window in Jena, but there are few of us ordinary mortals who can drive the obsessing questions from our minds as two fundamental ideologies lock in earth-shaking military ordeal.

In addition, there were official duties to perform, in the classroom and in the recruiting of officer material for the armed services. Election statistics are drab, indeed, under such conditions. The results of the study might have turned out better under different conditions, but I make no apology for them. They represent a moral and, in a sense, a mental travail.

My curiosity was originally aroused at the most contradictory ideological data to be found in the election returns. Of course, we in the field of political theory had, for years, emphasized the fact that ours is a non-ideological system of politics, a system that features the ins and the outs, the Government and the Opposition. We had noted the coalitions which developed at the Congressional level when vital issues were decided in legislative divisions; but in the constituencies the most amazing ideological discrepancies materialize. For instance, one might find a Republican and Democratic fusion candidate battling against a representative of a splinter party, even though the general election was essentially a struggle between the Republicans and the Democrats. Or one might find a Democratic-Socialist or a Republican-Socialist candidate; or the usual Democratic-Populist combination might be countered by a Republican-Populist-Democratic union in the next constituency.

The answer to this apparent contradiction is that the single-member constituency is a unit within itself. Opportunism plays as important a role there as it does in the state or in the United States at large. We play our politics to win, and our tactics, within the limits of decent precedents, are developed for the purpose of sending our representatives to Washington. I am fully conscious that this feature of our politics has not been properly emphasized in this book.

On the other hand, there are several conclusions which are, I believe, prerequisite to a thorough understanding of American politics. The effect of the control of the House of Representatives upon an impending presidential election has never been sufficiently stressed; nor have the sectional aspects of winning control of the House. Also, the waning and waxing strength of the two great parties in Congressional districts has not been the subject of elaboration. Finally, the effect of third parties at this level of our politics has received entirely too little attention.

I must briefly acknowledge credit to the many persons from state officials to congressmen and national administrative officers who have aided me in securing specific election returns.

I am further indebted to James Foliart and Wayne Quinlan for their painstaking work in the preparation of the data sheets, to William Oden for his endless hours with the comptometer, to Quintelle Reynolds for the careful typing of the manuscript from my scribbled hieroglyphics, and to S. C. Holland and Travis L. Scott for the preparation of the graphs. It is my simple hope that with all of the labor which has gone into these few pages of print, a little better understanding of our representative democracy will be achieved.

CORTEZ A. M. EWING

Norman, Oklahoma
May 8, 1947

Contents

I. Growth of the Congress   3

II. The Modern Party Battle   20

III. Popular Support of Major Parties   30

IV. The Battle in the Constituencies   49

V. Third Parties and Splinters   62

VI. Evaluation of the Plurality System   79

Index   105

Graphs

I. Party Membership in House, 1896–1944   27

II. Popular Vote Totals by Years and Parties   33

III. Popularity of National Tickets by Years   47

IV. Percentage of Seats Won by Majority Vote   53

V. Average Party Record by Percentage Categories   58

VI. Third-party Percentages by Years   67

Tables

Sectional Representation   19

Congressional Percentage of Presidential Vote   19

Efficiency of National Ticket   19

Seats Receiving Less than 0.5 Per Cent Vote   57

Percentage Receiving Less than 0.5 Per Cent Vote   57

Percentage of Seats Needed for Control   57

Percentage of Seats Won by Each Party   57

Percentage of Majority Won by Each Party   57

Seats Won in the East, 1896 to 1944   83

Party Success in the Border States   83

Party Success in the South   91

Party Success in the Middle West   91

Party Success in the West   91

Seats Earned and Won   97

CONGRESSIONAL ELECTIONS
1896-1944

Growth of the Congress

T HE CONGRESS of the United States is one of the historic legislative bodies of the last two thousand years. Though only one and one-half centuries have elapsed since its establishment, it will rank in history with the "Mother of Parliaments" in Britain and with the Roman legislative institutions as the most pronouncedly successful in the formulation of the popular will in legislative enactment. The efficacy of a lawmaking body depends not so much upon the importance of its state in the international community as upon its unbroken continuity. That it survives is proof of its success as an institution. Both the Roman and British legislative bodies were powerful instruments in the creation and organization of great empires. The Congress of the United States has earned its reputation as the consolidator of peoples inhabiting a land of continental proportions, of great natural and human diversity, and of a federal governmental organization which tends, at best, to foster sectional or local allegiances.

At its inception, the Congress was regarded as the fundamental organ of the central government. The lawmaking branch is the primary organ of democracy, whether it be representative or direct democracy, for in the legislative branch the popular will is translated into laws for the protection of the body politic. The executive authority administers these laws and the courts review the techniques of the administrative officers in the light of the intentions of the collective legislator. In this common governing process, the executive and the judge perform their functions after the legislature has acted. If there were no laws, there would be no president or judge, and the perfect anarchy would exist. However, since human society exists only through

3

the formulation and enforcement of common rules for human behavior, there is little gained through the discussion of the dynamics of philosophical anarchy.

It is necessary to state at the outset that the Congress was created to exercise specific powers which were delegated to it in the Constitution. The scope of its authority is, therefore, not comparable to that of the British Parliament. Throughout our short history there have been those who have deprecated the increasing usurpation by the Congress of powers that were presumed to have been reserved to the states in 1789. Some have inaccurately attributed to changed political thinking, as revealed in the amendments, the serious modification of our original federalism.[1] It should be noted that, except for the sixteenth amendment, little power has been delegated to Congress since 1789.[2] The real increase in the importance of national law in recent years has derived from the exercise of powers originally delegated but not utilized until the maturity of our industrial civilization made their exercise popularly desirable.

That Congress is quite different now from what it was in 1790, both in physical accoutrement and in its exercise of power, is self-evident. In the earlier era, people were generally fearful of governmental tyranny. The spectacular tyrannies of the world, the threats to the democratic life, were political in character.[3] It is not surprising, therefore, that the early Congresses

[1] For instance, see John T. Flynn, *Meet Your Congress* (New York, Doubleday, Doran, 1944), 126, 127. He maintains that there has been an "enormous extension of federal power," in late years; what he really intended to say, I presume, is that latent powers of the national government have in late years been utilized for the first time. We should make a distinction between utilization and usurpation.

[2] Of course, the eighteenth amendment substantially increased the power of Congress, but that power was recalled in the twenty-first amendment.

[3] This point of view remains with us still in such a work as Friedrich A. Hayek, *The Road to Serfdom* (Chicago, University of Chicago Press, 1944). The chief error, in the writer's opinion, which gives birth to books of this character is the assumption that political tyranny is the chief or only important species of the genus of human tyranny.

4

were not disposed to interfere, to any marked degree, with the popularly sacerdotalized area of individual liberty. But individual discretion for one may mean slavery for many. In our own times, the Congress, in common with parliaments all over the world, has invaded these fields of traditional human liberty and has defined new relationships for the protection of national human resources.

Our original Congressional organization featured a popularly elected House of Representatives and a Senate chosen by state legislatures. The fact that the latter was not selected by voters is telling evidence that the "fathers" did not trust immediate democratic decision. Men like Alexander Hamilton feared that popular election would inject passions and prejudices which would not be conducive to long-range solution of political problems. Even the franchise was seriously restricted. Ignorance and lowly economic position were deemed proof of political inability. The floodgates of democracy emitted only a very thin stream. The American democracy of 1800 was definitely of the middle-class character. Man must still be protected from his own lack of understanding. Even Thomas Jefferson cannot, according to our modern definition, be classified as a rabble-rouser, though Hamilton and others of his ilk regarded the Virginian and his sponsorship of the average husbandman as politically dangerous.

Since it was not popularly elected until after the adoption of the seventeenth amendment (1913), the Senate falls outside the scope of this study. We are here primarily interested in the dynamics of democratic choice—not so much in the product of Congressional effort as in the operation of the party system and the overall evaluation of the House of Representatives by the voters.

The size of the original house stands as an index to the general opinion in 1787 on the relative importance of the central government. The "fathers" agreed upon a yardstick that resulted in the more popular branch of Congress' having only 65 members.

Several of the states had much larger assemblies; for instance, the New York lower house had 70 members, while South Carolina elected 202 state representatives.

That the first house was small, in contrast to the lower houses of state legislatures, is not alone proof that the political leaders of the last quarter of the eighteenth century had little faith in representative democracy. It also indicates that these men, trained in state politics and attuned to the political mores of their states, regarded the state governments as of primary importance. The central government was viewed as an experiment, the success of which was as yet undetermined. Even after the new government was apparently well on the way to establishing itself as a permanent and important addition to our political institutions, prominent men like John Jay, the first chief justice of the Supreme Court, resigned to become candidates for election to important state offices. With a perspective created by 150 years of progressively increasing importance of the central government, we are inclined to substitute the contemporary view for that which existed at the beginning of our history as a federal state. There is every reason to believe that, if the "fathers" had envisaged the expanding role of the Congress, they might well have provided for a larger House of Representatives. However, with immaculate foresight, they permitted the lawmakers of the future to determine the size of future lower houses.

The procedure for determination of the size of the House is set forth in Article I, Section 2, of the Constitution. The "fathers" plainly intended that the House should be reapportioned once every ten years, or after each federal decennial census. The sixteenth census was taken in 1940, but there have been but fifteen apportionments. The Congress failed to reapportion after the census of 1920, that of 1910 being continued in effect for its second decennial period.

From 1790 to 1930 each of the thirteen apportionments, except that of 1840, increased the size of the preceding House.[4] The table on page 19 shows the almost continuously rising trend in membership from 1788 to 1912.[5] Not all of this precipitous rise can be accounted for through added representatives from the original thirteen states. Thirty-five new states were admitted to the Union during that period, and, though their original representations did not materially affect the size of the House, their rapid population growth was a dominant factor.

The increase in population led, no doubt, to an increase in the size of the House. If new states had not been admitted to the Union, and if the population increase had been proportionate in the thirteen original states, the membership of the House might have been kept at a small figure. States suffer a severe blow to their pride when their Congressional representation is officially reduced, a feeling that was the chief factor which prevented a reapportionment in 1920. For example, if the House had remained at the sixty-five–member size, the commonwealth of Virginia would today have but one representative. Her first delegation comprised ten representatives; today she has nine.[6]

The attempt to soften the blows against state pride, incidental in the loss of representation, resulted, then, in a modern house that is more than six and one-half times larger than the original one of 1788. The national average population quota for each apportionment is shown on the next page.

The admission of new states and the population growth in particular sections warred continually against the possibility of keeping the House small. By 1820 the national government had become important in the eyes of the politicians. The older gen-

[4] Technically, that of 1860 reduced by one the size of the preceding House, but the Congress in a supplemental bill added eight new members before the elections of 1862, thus actually increasing the House by seven members. However, since the seceding states were unrepresented in Washington, the 1862 election sent fewer representatives to Congress than had any election since 1810.

[5] See table on page 19.

[6] Virginia reached her highest mark in the apportionment of 1810, when she was allocated twenty-three representatives. She has declined steadily from that peak, never losing more than two in any apportionment, except that of 1840 in which she lost six.

7

Year	Number	% Increase	Year	Number	% Increase
1790	34,437		1870	134,684	6.20
1800	34,680	0.71	1880	151,906	12.79
1810	36,432	5.05	1890	173,901	14.48
1820	42,112	15.59	1900	193,426	11.23
1830	49,620	17.83	1910	210,328	8.74
1840	71,338	43.77	[1920	241,864	14.99]
1850	93,330	30.83	1930	280,675	16.05
1860	126,824	35.89	1940	301,164	7.30

eration which had created the Constitution was gone; the new one was not so imbued with state particularism. The last serious attempt to keep the House small came in 1840, when the Congress reduced the size from 240 to 223, thereby increasing the national quota by almost 44 per cent. However, this attempt was partly frustrated through the admission of four new states with seven representatives before the apportionment of 1850.[7]

A glance at the figures reveals the steady increase in size of the national quotas. In each of the fifteen apportionments, an increase is shown, though the greatest growth was from 1820 to 1860. The 16 per cent rise in 1930 was the largest since the Civil War. Population experts predict that our national population, omitting the possibility of acquiring new peoples through annexation of additional areas, will level off after 1960. If this is true, we have achieved approximately the maximum quota size, and we may well focus our attention upon the most efficient size for our national House of Representatives. If we had increased it to the size of the British House of Commons, the national quota with our 1940 population would have been but 213,018, or a reduction of 29.3 per cent of our present quota.[8]

The increase in quota from 1790 has now approached the figure of almost 775 per cent; or to put it more graphically, if the 1790 quota had been applied in the 1940 apportionment, our

[7] Texas, Iowa, Wisconsin, and Florida.

[8] These figures are based upon the 615-membership size of the Commons. That number has now been increased to 640, which alteration may well have some influence in this country in regard to the size of our future lower houses.

present house would have 38,042 members. This is an absurd figure, according to our present political thinking. Legislative bodies should be small enough to permit individual attention to legislative matters. With a deliberative body so large, there would be even greater difficulty than we now experience in attaching responsibility to the representatives. Likewise, the problem of providing physical accommodations for the legislative labors of a number such as this would appear more than merely difficult. Besides, the legislative process is generally regarded as necessitating a meeting of minds, a compromising of conflicting opinions, an achievement which would then be very difficult, if not impossible. Under such circumstances a wag might properly observe that, under present practice, the franking privilege would constitute an onerous burden upon the postal service!

The sectional aspects of American politics have intrigued many scholars. Sectionalism has been one of the chief factors in our national history, serving both for progressive and for restrictive ends. North-South or East-West dichotomies are as prominent as conservative-liberal divisions in our Congress. I have used five sections in earlier studies of American politics.[9] They are East, Border, South, Middle West, and West.[10] There are unanswerable objections to this sectional classification, as indeed there are to any attempted division. For instance, Oklahoma might as reasonably be included in the Border states as in the South; but if she were placed in the former category, equally strong reasons would demand her inclusion among the Southern states. The difficulty arises from the fact that the people of individual states may, upon specific questions, differ from the pre-

[9] See my *Supreme Court Judges 1789–1937* (Minneapolis: University of Minnesota Press, 1938), 124 and *Presidential Elections* (Norman: University of Oklahoma Press, 1940), *xiv*, 226.

[10] This classification puts New England, New York, New Jersey, and Pennsylvania in the East; Delaware, Maryland, West Virginia, Kentucky, and Missouri in the Border; the eleven secession states and Oklahoma in the South; Ohio, Indiana, Illinois, Iowa, Michigan, Wisconsin, and Minnesota in the Middle West; and the remaining fifteen states in the West.

vailing sectional point of view. It is the problem of the minority all over again, a problem that is difficult to solve where the majority, of whatever geographic designation, is presumed to speak for the whole. No organization, political or otherwise, can expect to realize an intellectual unanimity. There are minorities in Middletown, in the Faith Tabernacle, in the local unions of carpenters, and in the Parent-Teachers Association, as well as in the British Empire, in India, and in Bengal.

The sectional aspects of the apportionment policy are important. The East has, from the first, exceeded all sections in representation. Despite the fact that seven of its nine states were charter members of the Union, its population growth has kept it ahead of the South, where only four of twelve were among the thirteen original states. However, it should be remembered that one-third of the Negro slaves were not counted for representation, and thus the representation of the Southern states suffered. The sudden jump in the South's membership in 1872 derived from the operation of the thirteenth amendment and the utilization of the total population for apportionment purposes. The census of 1860 showed the total national slave population to be 3,952,801, an increase of 748,724 over the census figure of 1850. In 1860, the eleven Southern states had 3,520,116 and the four Border states had 429,441 slaves.[11] If one-third of Southern slaves had been added to the apportionment population in 1860, the South would have had seventy congressmen (rather than the sixty-one allotted it) as compared to the eighty-four given to the nine Eastern states in the first 1860 apportionment.[12] The four Border states would have picked up but one member if their total slave population had been counted for apportionment purposes.

In 1850 the eleven Southern states were deprived of ten seats

[11] In addition, there were 3,244 slaves in District of Columbia and in three territories—Nebraska, Utah, and New Mexico.

[12] Eight congressmen were added to the original apportionment of 1860, three of whom went to Eastern states.

by the two-thirds constitutional provision. This would have given that section seventy-six to the East's ninety-two. Incidentally, from 1850 to 1860, the slave population increased only 23.4 per cent, while the whole population increased 34.7 per cent, and the non-slave population 36.6 per cent.

The conspicuous differential between the increase in slave and non-slave populations may well serve to explain the development of a particularistic political psychology in the South after 1850; for of that section's 9,103,332 total population, 38.7 per cent were Negro slaves whose increase in the past decade had been slightly less than two-thirds (64 per cent) of the percentage increase of the non-slave population. Since the other sections, except the Border, were composed wholly of non-slave people, the political prospects of the future were not too bright in the South. The section was being slowly swallowed by birth in, and immigration into, the East and the Middle West.

The tendency of political dynamics to retain or increase the representation of a section and, therefore, with expanding settlement and population to increase the size of the House, is shown in the record of the East. That section's number of representatives reached 97 in 1812; and in the past 133 years, its house total has fluctuated between a low of 92 and a high of 123, between a loss of 5 per cent and a gain of 27 per cent. In those years, the House increased from 181 to 435 members. Even within the section, the purely agrarian states found their population shifting into the industrial centers. This was especially true of all New England states except Rhode Island and Massachusetts.[13] The gains were chalked up by New York and New Jersey. Pennsylvania just about held her own in the transition from agrarian to industrial society.

In the Border marches, the story is one of expansion. Missouri was admitted in 1820; and that section of Virginia now known

[13] The reduction in Massachusetts house seats from twenty (1816) to thirteen (1822) resulted from the admission of a portion of Massachusetts as the state of Maine.

as West Virginia withdrew from the South during the Civil War. These two new states account largely for the increase in sectional representation of twenty (1812) to forty (1912).

The South has already been partially discussed. On the whole, it has been an expanding section, with a birth rate higher than the national average. Since the Civil War, a principal article of export has been population. Its most marked increase after 1900 has come from the phenomenal population growth in Texas and Oklahoma, as these two states, not members of the Union in 1840, now contribute one-fourth of the entire sectional representation. Like Kentucky (Border), the older agrarian states east of the Mississippi lost representation, because their population increase lagged behind the national average.[14] For instance, the three states of the upper South—Virginia, North Carolina, and Tennessee—lost 28.6 per cent of their 1820 representation before 1920; and South Carolina surrendered one-third of her 1820 figure.

However, this historic trend ends in the emergence of the "New South," as Henry Grady and others like him called it. The coming of industry to this historically agricultural South has retained and developed pools of population which have in the past two decades placed the South as the second most populous section. North Carolina, Florida, and Tennessee received increased representation for the 1942 elections. Most observers predict that the last named state will move up markedly under the TVA. Tobacco processing and textile manufacturing were largely responsible for North Carolina's increase, and recreation for Florida's.

The prospects are that larger percentages of the abundant natural resources will be exploited within the section, especially cotton and rayon textiles, vegetable oils, and timber and tobacco products, as well as the hundreds that come from coal, iron, mica, bauxite, and petroleum. In fact, the scientific utilization

[14] This region saw little immigration from Europe, largely on account of its predominant agrarian character.

of petroleum may mark the next era's spectacular extension in chemical engineering.

The freight-rate differentials have, in the past, fostered the establishment of small processing plants in the section, but they have militated against the development of industry upon a larger scale. If those differentials are removed, the entire industrial picture of this erstwhile "colonial" section will be substantially altered, and for the first time in more than a hundred years the South may gain population at the expense of the other areas.

For the hundred years after 1800 the development of the Middle West was the most important factor in the building of the United States as a strong world power. Starting with a purely frontier, agrarian economy, especially after the Civil War, it moved to the fore as an industrial rival to the East. The culmination of that pronounced trend came in the exploitation of the great iron-ore resources of the Superior region and the establishment of the motor industry in and around Detroit. That city became the principal assembly point for the motor industry. Hundreds of cities and towns of the region contributed their specialized parts to the motor mechanism. The section grew apace, and that growth was reflected in intensive agriculture and especially in the rapid increase of dairy products. From 1803 to 1940 every reapportionment gave additional representation to the Middle West. However, in 1940 the section lost four seats to the more rapidly growing Pacific coast West.

The intra-section story follows the national pattern. The preponderantly agricultural areas lost Congressional seats to the industrial centers. Thus, the same factors which changed the national scene so much were at work within the section. Michigan and Illinois grew rapidly; Ohio, Wisconsin, and Minnesota increased approximately at the national rate; but Indiana and Iowa lost over one-fifth of their house seats between 1902 and 1942. However, the relative decline in those states was conspicuously less than in purely agrarian states such as Nebraska and Kansas.

More than any of the other sections, the West epitomized the typically American process of agricultural extension. It is still young. Following California, its first states—Kansas and Nevada—were admitted to the Union during the Civil War. Since then, twelve other states (six between 1888 and 1895) have qualified for admission. The section is now complete, unless definitions may be altered to include future states of Alaska, Hawaii, or Oceana. Between the Civil War and World War I, the agrarian infiltration into new areas was steady though not sufficient to influence the representation picture for the whole country. The size of the House was increased slightly through the new admissions, but the growth in industrial states was sufficient to maintain their positions of political power. Some of the older agrarian states kept their seats, but lost relatively through the increasing size of the House. In 1902, the thirteen states of the West sent only thirty-nine congressmen to Washington. These constituted less than 10 per cent of the whole House. However, by 1942 the West had increased its representation by more than 60 per cent.

The early history of the United States featured the clash between the two dominant sections—the East and the South. Since the Civil War, the battle of the "isms" has lain underneath the political surface. But the great issue grew out of the question: How far shall the government go in bringing the good life to the common man? In contrast to the earlier period, this political question divides the people of every section into "pro" and "con" groups. It is, therefore, an ideological rather than a purely sectional issue.

The Civil War ended one era and initiated another. Most scholars today, I gather, feel that the "irrepressible conflict" was not nearly so inevitable as earlier historical research presented it; that the perfection of democratic procedures could have prevented the outbreak of hostilities, the subsequent loss of man power, and the accentuation of bitterness between the sections. Had there been no Civil War the economic losses would have been far less for the South if the slaves had been freed without compensation to the owners. Even the free sections would have profited if owners had been doubly compensated for every manumitted slave.

The nineteenth century was to prove throughout the Western world that political control was the best means for effecting social reform. Always potent in politics, traditionalism was found by its defenders to solve few public controversies. The age of reason, through American interpreters like Jefferson and Paine, presented a new basis for political decision. That which had been was not sacred merely because it had occupied an honorable place in the stream of human history. Issues were raised upon what ought to be.

The East, joined first by the energetic Middle West and then by the swaddling West, applied the test of reason to the slavery question. Of course, there were both economic and moral bases for this political development. Defending its economic and social system, and rationalizing a moral code for that purpose, the South stood not too unanimously, but nevertheless clamorously, in defense of constitutional traditionalism. The philosophizing of John C. Calhoun epitomizes this defense in its highest and purest form. No other Southerner approached him in marshaling logic to the problem of political particularism. It matters not, for our purposes here, that his philosophy was undemocratic and clearly antithetical to the main currents of American political thought. It is enough that his doctrines of Negro incapacity and the basis for slavery in natural law were accepted by the "slavocracy" as immutable.

In the first Congress, the not-too-free East had almost 54 per cent of the House members. In no congress until the outbreak of the Civil War did the free sections have less than that percentage. The extension of the philosophy of freedom into the Northwest Territory doomed the interests of slavery. Thus Thomas Jefferson's program for the elimination of slavery was ultimately successful, even though he was never to know that this would be the case. Geography was on the side of freedom. The slavocracy leaders were not concerned so long as the settlement of lands west of the southern Appalachians and the Blue Ridge progressed at a rate approximate to that in the old Northwest Territory. Their interests could be protected through the admission of slave states, and thus equal strength could be maintained in the Senate, even though the House was slowly slipping from their control.

The Missouri Compromise (1820) was an attempt to perpetuate this equal status in the Senate, but it was, in fact, a defeat for the slavery interests. It left the major portion of unsettled territory in the free category. The twelve Border and Southern states at that time had only 43 per cent of the House membership, and the apportionment for the election of 1822 reduced it by a percentage point. Alabama, Mississippi, Louisiana, and Missouri were already admitted. In the next twenty years, only two states were admitted—Arkansas and Michigan. The balance was still kept in the Senate, but the slavocracy's House strength had dropped another point. In the next decade, Florida and Texas matched Iowa and Wisconsin, but the Kansas and Minnesota territories were on the agenda for rapid development and the South had no immediate prospect for new slave states. The Mexican War and the acquisition of our Hispanic Southwest and the settlement of the Oregon question brought into the public domain the prospect of future states in numbers almost equal to the thirty already in the Union.

The demand of California for admission, a demand that could not well be denied after the migration of so many Americans there following the gold strike, furnished the *coup de grâce* for the old Missouri Compromise tactics of the Southern leaders. Geography and the vagaries of international politics had nullified their statesmanship of an earlier generation. They must now fight to extend slavery anywhere, regardless of their promises that land north of "thirty-six, thirty" would be free territory. The North sensed victory; California would break the stalemate in the Senate; and the forces of freedom could battle those of slavery in the territories. The Democratic party, trying to compromise the great issue, found itself pledged to the "squatter sovereignty" of Stephen A. Douglas, and the Kansas-Nebraska Act became national law.

In the first house elected under the apportionment of 1850, the slave states had but 38 per cent of the seats. The sands were running out for slavery. The main battle which had heretofore been fought in Washington, the battle between the forces of freedom and traditionalism, was shifted to the territories. And the Civil War may be said to have begun in the Territory of Kansas in the early fifties. Backed by money and influence from the North, John Brown made human liberty a holy crusade, even though it was a violent one. The vanguard of the slave interests were poured as missionaries of the South into the new territory; they were as violent as the fanatics who followed the leadership of Brown. Violence broke out; each side sought to exterminate the other; cities were sacked; men were shot down in cold blood for no other reason than political conviction. The story of "Bloody Kansas," with only a Hellenization of place names might be included in a history of the Greek struggles between the Macedon and anti-Macedon parties before the birth of Christ.

Slavery lost the battle in Washington. And it was fast losing the battle in Kansas before the memorable election of 1860. Its leaders had but two choices: they could surrender to the inevitable political decision and await the inevitable manumission of their slaves, or they could break the bonds of the Union and perpetuate their now sacerdotalized institutions in a separate political entity. The first choice necessitated a serious loss of face and the prospect of a minority position in national politics. It requires a really great statesmanship to face such personally displeasing political alternatives and, unfortunately for the whole United States, the South had not, at that time, a political leadership that could accurately be evaluated as more than mediocre.

The Rhetts, the Yanceys, and the Davises were little men. The political system of Calhoun had fallen about the ears of his successors. The great South Carolinian had overpraised his southland in his desire to coalesce and discipline his political followers. The results were similar to those in every country where emotionalism replaces the normal natural basis of politics. Population in the free states destroyed the cause of slavery. Occupying a favored position, the North was in no mood to surrender to the demands of the South. One may refer to this as the tyranny of the majority, as John Stuart Mill was wont to do, but it is still a dominant force in democratic society. It is well-nigh impossible to overawe self-conscious majorities. And the Southern threat of force was no more than the last desperate effort of a dying cause to retain its power and its institutional integrity.

Note 5, *page 7.*

SECTIONAL REPRESENTATION
1788–1944

Section	1788	1790	1800	1810	1820	1830	1840	1850	1860	1870	1880	1890	1900	1910	1930	1940
East	35	57	76	97	105	112	94	92	87	95	95	99	108	123	122	120
Border	7	11	16	20	23	24	22	24	27	33	36	37	39	40	35	35
South	23	37	49	58	67	75	68	66	61	73	85	90	98	112	111	113
Middle West			1	6	18	29	41	50	64	81	90	96	102	107	108	104
West								2	6	10	19	34	39	53	59	63
U. S.	65	105	142	181	213	240	225	234	245	292	325	356	386	435	435	435

PARTY'S CONGRESSIONAL PERCENTAGE OF PARTY'S PRESIDENTIAL VOTE

	1896	1900	1904	1908	1912	1916	1920	1924	1928	1932	1936	1940	1944
Republican	94.5	94.8	91.2	92.4	135.2	93.0	88.9	93.5	65.1	88.8	102.1	96.3	97.6
Democrat	86.5	96.4	104.9	102.0	99.0	85.0	99.0	127.4	95.1	81.1	86.1	89.2	91.8

EFFICIENCY OF NATIONAL TICKET

	1896	1900	1904	1908	1912	1916	1920	1924	1928	1932	1936	1940	1944	Av.
Republican	99.4	99.1	102.9	101.6	69.5	100.9	105.6	100.4	144.2	105.8	91.9	97.5	96.2	101.2
Democrat	108.6	97.4	89.5	92.1	94.9	110.5	94.9	73.7	98.8	115.8	109.1	105.3	102.3	99.4

The Modern Party Battle

MODERN party politics in the United States are said to have begun in 1896. The date is purely arbitrary. There are equally strong reasons for using 1876 as the initial date; more than a decade had elapsed since the battle of Appomattox; the Democratic party was able to put a formidable national ticket in the field and to receive the support of practically one-half of the electorate; the party had, except in Republican ranks, ceased to be the "party of treason" and had become, to all practical purposes, the potential alternative to Republican hegemony.

But these twenty years from Tilden to Bryan were years of national political instability. It may be said that they were the years in which the old agrarian party system was living on borrowed time. It had no more than illusory solutions for the problems which were created by the rise of the new industrialism. Of course, it must not be inferred that the parties faced the real issues after Cleveland's second administration. Many campaigns were to come and go before the control of economic corporations was to become a principal issue between parties and, thereafter, to find a place in the convention resolutions of both major parties.

These were years when the new industrial strategists were leaving the older agrarians at the post, and the latter had no more grasp of the situation than to demand that they, too, should be privileged to run with their teeth in the wind. The liberalism of this period was expressed by the young Bryan when he declared pontifically that the operator of the crossroads general store was as much a businessman as the banker on Wall Street. The "boy orator of the Platte" may, with his definition of "businessman," have been correct, but the dynamics of the era gave much greater leverage to the directors of trusts and combines than to the small, independent economic entrepreneurs.

These were the years when our legislative policy looked to the curbing of the selfish, materialistic economic interests through the cheapening of money, through legal prohibition of "conspiracies in unreasonable restraint of interstate trade," through publication of the facts of unfair trade practices, and through the marshaling of enraged public moral conscience to deter malpractitioners. And these were the years too when the dynamics of the new industrialism were beginning to be understood by those in charge of potentially powerful economic forces. Once fully understood, these hard facts were to find logical expression in the trustification of American industry. After the turn of the century, this process was to proceed apace, despite the moral indignation of the muckrakers and the protagonists of laissez-faire liberalism.

There is little doubt that the public, frozen here in the social and intellectual lag which accompanies all fundamental transformations of social institutions, sensed the threat to the "great society." The exposures of Steffens, Myers, Ida Tarbell, Russell and others were avidly consumed by an enlarged reading public. That the public sense of justice was violated is shown by the popularity of *McClure's Magazine* during the first decade of the new century. But, withal, on either side of the great controversy there were few who really understood the inevitable doom of the traditionally moral agrarian order. Out of the social imponderables would have to come a political policy for the achievement of reasonable security for the common man, or the entire order of American democracy would go into the discard.

Social democracy in industrial European countries had embraced the Marxist materialism, but it was at that time little more than an intellectual protest to the trend toward economic centralization. In 1900 the social democratic movement made its first appearance in American national politics, with a program far less radical than that offered by the American Socialist Labor party. But these were only splinters on the great timber of American protest. The American liberal was an individualist, an inveterate believer in the idea that bigness was synonymous with immorality, and that the most reasonable solution of this new threat to people's liberty was to remove the economic malignancies and to adopt a national policy not conducive to the development of the wild cells of industrial organization. Somehow, however, the achievement of this return to agrarian morality was to be realized without the utilization of the immoral instrument of governmental intervention, or at least not through the conscious creation of the government as a constant and alert guardian of the public interest. The agrarians were equally fearful of tyrannical government and exploitative economics, and they were in no mood to create a second danger to overcome a first one. This is the imponderable element in the modern period of American politics.

We have selected the modern period for our analysis of the party basis of Congress for another reason. The two-party system reached its maturity. It functioned in a non-ideological manner. Only in the memories of older people was the Republican party the champion of human liberty or the Democratic party the defender of chattelship in human flesh. Each was plotting a practical program upon which it could appeal to the public and—God and the people willing—capture control of the government and save the country from certain ruin under the other's immediate direction.

The returns for Congressional elections are also more reliable for this latter period than for the earlier ones. When parties were counting their own votes, there was, at least, the basis for honest and other errors. We might have gone back for ten or fifteen years before 1896 without too much inconvenience and without too great hazard to accuracy of data, but fifty years (and twenty-five elections) should give us a fair picture of the major forces in the Congressional aspects of American politics.

In the Congress elected in 1894, the Republicans overthrew the Democratic majority. Grover Cleveland, a Democrat, was president; Thomas Reed, a Republican, was speaker of the House of Representatives. This contradiction to the theory of responsible government happens fairly often under the American system of "government by the calendar." The Republican prospects were rising, after a period of twelve years in which liberal members of the party, or mugwumps, had followed a practice of bolting the party ticket in order to force liberalization of the party program.

In the period from 1896 to 1944, the Republicans won seven presidential elections, the Democrats six. In the twenty-five Congresses of the same period, the Republicans won fourteen, and the Democrats eleven.[1] This is an unusually even distribution of party success. In no other period of our history have the two parties battled on practically even terms over so long a stretch. And yet the variations within the half-century were at times very great. For instance, in 1936 the Republicans elected but 90 members of the House (20.7 per cent); in 1920, the Democrats received only 136 seats (31.3 per cent). On account of the preponderant Democratic convictions of the South, that party will, in times of party adversity, elect more congressmen than will the Republicans in their leanest years. There are fewer safe seats for the Republicans than for the Democrats.

During the fifty years 1894 to 1944, there were four switches from one major party to another in the national administration; from the Democrats to the Republicans in 1896 and 1920, and vice-versa in 1912 and 1932. Preceding each of these switches, the control of the House of Representatives had passed from the administration to the opposition. In fact, not since 1888 has a national party won a presidential election without having had a

[1] This count lists the 1930 election as a Republican victory, even though the Democrats were able to organize the House. If organization of the House were the criterion, the record would stand as thirteen for the Republicans and twelve for the Democrats.

majority in the House in the preceding biennium. And in that presidential election (1888), the losing Democrats received more popular votes than did the winning Republicans.

Thus the precedents of the past half-century delineate an important law of American politics: *Success in a presidential election will go to that party which already has majority control of the House of Representatives.* No serious scholar would imply that this precedent is unbreakable, any more than that the anti-third-term tradition was inviolable. But until it is broken, it remains a fairly reliable criterion for the interpretation of American politics. No doubt situations might arise in which political opinion would shift more rapidly than it has since 1888. Emergencies by their very nature present abnormal political conditions. By way of illustration, most observers believe that the emergency of 1940 was a more deciding factor in the re-election of Franklin D. Roosevelt for a third term than was any popular departure from the anti-third-term conviction. The same situation existed in 1944, when Mr. Roosevelt was elected for a fourth time. However, in these campaigns, two firmly entrenched principles of American democracy came into direct conflict—one, the fear that a single leader would, consciously or unconsciously, take unto himself power that rightfully belonged in other branches of our government or in the people; the other, that, in a time of emergency, it is needlessly dangerous to experiment with untried leadership. This latter fear was succinctly expressed in the campaigns of 1916, 1940, and 1944 in the admonition, "Don't change horses in the middle of the stream."

In 1916 the House-control precedent came very near to being smashed. The Republicans almost won the presidential election. It was our closest national contest in recent years. In 1912 the Republican party had been split asunder by the internecine struggle between liberals and conservatives. By 1916 that breach was practically repaired. In the 1914 Congressional elections, the Republicans won sixty-five Democratic seats and reduced the Democratic margin to only thirty votes.

The "Revolt of 1910" paved the way for the Wilson victory in 1912. Under the leadership of the young George Norris, the Progressives and the Democrats had shorn the Republican Speaker, "Uncle Joe" Cannon, of his "dictatorial" powers.[2] And in the November elections of that year, the Republican membership dropped more than 20 per cent (from 215 to 168). The path was cleared for the election of a Democratic president. In 1918 the way was provided for the national Republican victory of 1920. The Democratic House membership was reduced from 214 to 182.

The Democratic control of the Seventy-first Congress (1931–33) derived largely from a fortuitous circumstance. The Republicans elected a majority, but the party was not united. There was considerable independence in many members who had pursued personal rather than party tactics in the election campaign. Some had voiced overt criticism of the Hoover administration. And, before the House met for the purposes of organization, sufficient vacancies occurred on the Republican side to reduce that party to less than the majority needed for the election of a speaker. However, the 18 per cent loss in membership from 1928 to 1930 proved to be a reliable portent of the tremendous party loss in 1932. In four years the Republicans lost 57 per cent of their House seats, falling from 267 in 1928 to 115 in 1932.

The fifty-year record, therefore, is that the party in control of the House of Representatives has not lost a presidential election, while the presidential administration has four times lost control of the House. And in each of the four cases, the party losing control of the House was defeated in the presidential election two years later.

There exists no way of determining whether this phenomenon of modern American politics has its origin in the slow altera-

[2] The insurgents alluded to Cannon's powers as "dictatorial" or "tyrannical"; the loyal Republicans described them as essentially "responsible."

25

tion of political allegiance, and the loss of House control merely exhibits a trend in citizen thinking that would, even with no off-year elections, reveal itself with compelling suddenness in the next presidential election; or whether the party in control of the House has an advantage in the campaign. Do congressmen assist substantially the vote-getting efforts of the presidential candidate of their party, so that a majority in the House would be more effective than a minority?

We have more often heard the opposite view, that the Congressional candidates merely made fast their holds upon the presidential coattails and thus rode into office. The precedents of the last half-century would seem to deny this explanation of congressmen's success, or at least to reduce it in importance. If that is the proper theory, why did it fail four times in the past thirteen presidential elections? In two of these four, a president was defeated for re-election. The obvious answer is that in neither 1912 nor 1932 would a Republican congressman's chances for re-election have been substantially improved through catching hold of the presidential coattail.

In those twenty-five Congressional elections, there were 10,415 contests decided. Of these, the Democrats won 5,301 and the Republicans 4,986. Third parties accounted for 128. Thus, though the Democrats won control of the House three fewer times than their opponents, they elected 315 more congressmen. These seats are accounted for by the larger number of safe seats controlled by the Democrats. Generally, the Democratic minority strength was greater than that of the Republicans during their minority years. The average minority strength was 167 for the Democrats and 164 for the Republicans, and it should be mentioned that seven of the Congresses in which the Democrats were in a minority came between 1896 and 1910, which was prior to the time when the House reached its maximum strength of 435. The party strength for the twenty-five Congresses is shown in Graph I.

A glance at the graph will immediately reveal two obvious

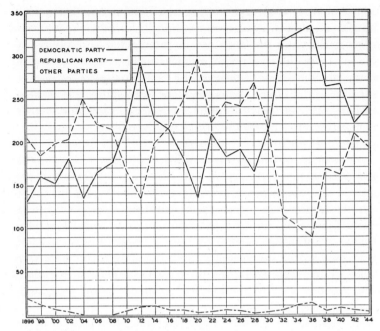

GRAPH I : *Party Membership in House,* 1896–1944

generalizations on the politics of the period. First, third parties have won but insignificant numbers of the House membership. This does not mean, as will be shown later, that third-party candidacies have not been important in determining the control of the House, for the presence of a non-major-party candidate in a constituency may well account for a congressman's election. But from the standpoint of sheer numbers, the Republicans and the Democrats have elected 10,287 congressmen, while minor parties have won but 128 seats. In 1896 and 1898, third parties elected nineteen and eleven members, respectively. In 1934 and 1936, they elected ten and twelve. The former were largely Populists or Fusionists; the latter were Progressives, Farmer-Laborites, American Laborites, or just plain independents. In three Congresses (1905, 1907, and 1909), there were no congressmen who were not nominally members of the two great parties, but this must not be interpreted as implying no dissent from the two major organizational programs. In fact, party labels are poor criteria indeed to judge the degree of conformity in the House. For there have been campaigns, such as that of 1912, in which Republicans were elected to Congress who refused to support the presidential candidate or the official program of the party.

The other obvious truth revealed in the graph is that, once in ascendancy, a party retains that advantage over a fairly long period. The Republicans kept House domination from 1895 to 1911 and from 1919 to 1931; the Democrats were the majority party from 1911 to 1919, and from 1931 to 1947. Thus, the extended periods of control are now equal for the two parties, with each having dominated an uninterrupted stretch of sixteen years. The graph, therefore, proves a basic pattern in American politics. The opposition will certainly come to power, but it takes a considerable period of time for a party to lose the confidence of a majority of the electorate. Our system of set elections reduces the opportunity for the minority to come into power, for in a parliamentary democracy, such as Great Britain, the opposition may capitalize upon temporary embarrassments of the government. In our country, it is merely accidental if an election campaign occurs during a political crisis.

This fact determines largely the character of our political campaigns. If the country is not in political crisis and there are no really pressing issues, apparent differences must be manufactured. Political blockbusters are rained upon the public. The people must be awakened! The country must be saved from purely imaginary perils. As a result, the landscapes of our election campaigns are more likely to be pastels than heavier and more dynamic colors. Generally, there is an atmosphere of artificiality, which no doubt contributes to lack of voter interest and to an increase in the influence of traditionalism in the voter support of party candidates. Also, if issues appear less than vital, the personalities of candidates become, for the independent voters, the principal element in political decision. Our presidential campaigns may, as some observers have remarked, become no more than personal popularity contests, and the voter appeals more comparable to the sales techniques of Hollywood than to the measured seriousness of Mr. Jefferson's virtuous husbandmen.

Our campaign orators, utilizing their matchless rhetoric for purely sophist ends, continue to remind our citizens that ours is a "government of laws and not of men." Laws are presumed to represent the collective interests in the welter of our conflicting atomistic society. Issues are, therefore, the basis for the refinement of those rules of common behavior. And controversy becomes the essential means for achieving the education and understanding necessary to the establishment of the emergent compromise, which is law. To conduct campaigns which ignore issues, or present merely fictitious ones, means, therefore, that the controversies and differences occur in the legislative halls rather than in the constituencies and renders undistinctive the party label as a criterion of a legislator's views upon political subjects. Therefore, we witness the phenomena of Democrat opposing Democrat, and Republican opposing Republican, on the floors of our national Congress.

The end result of this characteristic is to make it easier for a party to remain in power; for, in power, it becomes the recipient of the favors and support of powerful economic groups, while at the same time giving lip service to the principle of the "greatest good for the greatest number." When the latter is not, in the opinion of the greatest number, being achieved with reasonable celerity, the party leaders may point with confidence to the votes of congressmen, to the speeches of the faithful, and to the unequivocal approval expressed in the official party platform.

Popular Support of Major Parties

I N the twenty-five elections, more than 571,000,000 votes were cast for Congressional candidates. As these were the years in which vote totals rose to astronomical levels, the average of almost 23,000,000 for each election means very little. There are many factors which contributed to the phenomenal increase in the exercise of the suffrage. For instance, woman suffrage undoubtedly accounts for much of this accretion, but not for so much of it as has been assumed by some writers. A few of the states permitted women to vote throughout the fifty-year period. Others joined the ranks before World War I. And, with the adoption of the Nineteenth Amendment in 1920, women secured the franchise throughout the Union, and, thus, in denial of the rule of the paterfamilias, were given two votes where they only had one before! The newly enfranchised were quicker to develop the habit of voting in some sections than in others. The West and the Middle West showed the largest immediate gains, while the South exhibited little increase in 1920 and immediately thereafter.[1] That the West does not show a large increase from 1916 to 1920 was due to the fact that eleven of its fifteen states had adopted woman suffrage before the Nineteenth Amendment became effective for the entire United States.

Even without the potential doubling of the electorate through woman suffrage, the vote totals were rising. A prominent factor was the increase in population, both through large-

[1] The increases of 1920 over the 1916 totals for the sections were as follows: East, 62.9 per cent; Border, 69.5 per cent; South, 43 per cent; Middle West, 66.2 per cent; and West, 16.2 per cent. For a comparison of the sections in the presidential elections for the same years, see my *Presidential Elections*, 208, 209.

scale immigration and through natural population increase. Medical science was successfully combating many of the diseases which, through the nineteenth century, had assumed epidemic proportions. Especially had the diseases common to childhood and early maturity been brought under more effective control. As a result, the percentage of citizens over sixty years of age was greatly increased.

The continued advancements in medical science have caused many social scientists to advocate the lowering of the voting age from the old common-law standard of twenty-one to eighteen or some other tender age. They reason that the electorate is becoming top-heavy with those "whose futures are behind them" and who, therefore, are interested essentially in preserving the security of the *status quo* or, if capable of achieving it, of extending that security through legislation which threatens the vitality of our economic system. The ease with which old-age-pension amendments were added to state constitutions and the consequent burdens placed upon the taxpayers have brought many supporters of social legislation to fear that, in the competition with the drive for security, sufficient attention may not be given to the need for extending the opportunity for young people preparing to take their places in the nation's economic order.

A third factor in this vote increase arose in the national psychology. At the beginning of the period, the workers, for instance, paid far less attention to formal politics than they have since 1929. The American Federation of Labor was pledged to a nonpartisan policy. Thus, its leaders reasoned, the workers would be in position to bargain with whichever party came to power. However, the failure of economic tactics in the early twenties naturally caused labor to turn to politics.

A fourth factor was the increase in literacy in the country. Even without laws barring illiterate citizens from voting, the literate portion of the population will vote in larger percentages than the unlettered. Faced with the bewildering array of economic and political problems, the illiterate, following the road of least resistance, leave to their betters the task of extricating them. It is the old medieval formula, which placed reliance on quality.

There develops easily the spectre of social classification, which in itself acts as a deterrent to political interests among the lower classes. Is there anyone who holds much optimism for the emergence of democracy among the masses of India's teeming population? Democracy can operate successfully only where there is the will to express individual opinions, where there is sufficient confidence in the ability of the collectivity to find solutions for social problems, and where there is, above all, enough intellectual acumen to realize that these problems are largely of man's own creation rather than the dictum of an unmerciful natural law. If peoples accept degradation as the decree of nature, there is little that popular government can do for them, for their despoilers will only too gladly explain poverty as a natural dispensation, the will of God, and the testing formula for the nobler life hereafter. Obscurantism is the ready technique for those in power, for it secures their political positions and inflates their egoisms simultaneously.

Exhibiting many of the distinguishing marks of medieval society, the South has lagged far behind the other sections in the exercise of the suffrage. Moreover, there was little improvement in the recent Democratic years under the leadership of Franklin D. Roosevelt. The South was keenly agitated by the issues surrounding the great election of 1896. Mr. Bryan's appeal was to the underdog in the American economic and social order, and the eleven states of that section cast no less than three and one-half million votes for Congressional candidates. Even with the addition of Oklahoma to the section, it did not equal that figure again until 1928, when it was fearful that a lay member might become the first representative of Catholicism to succeed to the presidency. Poll taxes, white primaries, understanding clauses, grandfather's clauses, and threats and intimidation were

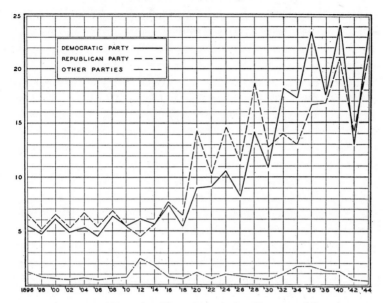

GRAPH II : *Popular Vote Totals by Years and Parties*

all used to deter voting among the Negroes and the low-income whites.

The defenders of suffrage restriction in the section seek always to leave the impression that the restrictions are aimed essentially at the Negroes, but the plain fact is that more whites are disfranchised than Negroes by these patently medieval political instruments.[2] The Congressional election statistics re-

[2] The 1928 and 1944 increases over the 1896 totals in Congressional votes for the various sections were:

	1928	1944
East	212.1%	302.4%
Border	132.9	139.1
South	2.2	39.9
Middle West	125.0	206.7
West	242.8	462.9
U. S.	130.5	208.3
U. S. minus South	270.6	360.8

33

veal an alarming disparity between the South and the remainder of the United States. The 1928 percentage increase over 1896 in the rest of the country was 123 times that in the South, while the 1944 increase over 1896 was in the rest of the country more than 9 times that in the South. If votes rather than percentages are taken, the South's increase was but three-tenths of 1 per cent and 4.6 per cent respectively, for the 1928 and 1944 increases over the 1896 total in the remainder of the United States. These figures reveal a tragic story in the failure of the South to ripen into the democratic conception of social control.

The Congressional election vote totals for parties and years are shown in Graph II. The Republicans were first in fifteen of the twenty-five elections, even though they were able to organize the House in but thirteen sessions. They failed to secure, or retain, the majority necessary to major-party status following the 1916, 1930, and 1942 elections, even though they had pluralities in each. The Democrats won a popular plurality in 1928, but failed to win a plurality of the House seats. A total of 571,-222,698 votes were cast in the twenty-five elections, with the Republicans getting 47.6 per cent, the Democrats 47.8 per cent, and third parties 4.5 per cent.[3] These figures reveal how evenly the two major parties have battled through the last half-century. At times, one has apparently smothered the other in an avalanche of votes, but always the other returned to power after years of performing the functions of opposition. Fourteen years was the longest stretch of victory for either of the major parties, the Republicans winning consistently from 1896 to 1908, inclusive. Again, beginning in 1918, the Republicans took seven consecutive elections; but the Democrats won six in the F.D.R. heyday.

The conspicuous characteristic of the graph is the serrated

[3] These figures include also the votes in at-large elections, but these have been reduced to the single-member constituency standard. Thus no at-large votes were counted in states where both single-member constituency and at large contests were simultaneously waged. At large totals in states where no single-member constituency contests occurred were reduced to the common standard.

lines which mark the party totals. This effect is the result of the smaller totals for off-year elections. The ballyhoo which has become so much a part of American presidential elections is without doubt responsible for the larger Congressional totals in presidential years. The average vote for the latter was 25,913,554, for the off-years only 19,528,873. This means that for every hundred votes cast in presidential years for Congressional candidates, only seventy-five are cast for such nominees in the off-year elections. Thus, the ballyhoo, the concerted efforts at getting out the vote, and the feeling that a president is more important than other officials brings more citizens to the polling places and increases the Congressional vote by one-third over that of the off-year elections.

In the two off-year elections conducted during wartime (1918 and 1942), the total vote fell far below the standards set during the normal peace years.[4] In neither of these elections were regular procedures provided for soldier voting. Only after extensive squabbling, which did little to enhance the declining popular esteem for Congress, was it possible to enact an ineffectual war services' voting law in time for the presidential election of 1944. The factor of total war affected the 1942 election much more than that of 1918. The mushroom war industries drew workers from all over the United States. Not only were those in the armed services unable to vote, but a high percentage of the great army of industrial workers, both men and women, were disqualified on the basis of residence qualifications. Incidentally, these disqualifications affected the Democrats vitally, for labor was preponderantly behind the Roosevelt program. For the first time since 1930, the total Republican vote was greater than that for the Roosevelt party.

The national trend is for the voters to pay less attention to

[4] In 1918, the total was but 76.6 per cent of the 1916 Congressional vote, and but 68.6 per cent of the presidential vote of that year. In 1942, the vote was but 60 per cent and 58.9 per cent of the Congressional and presidential totals of 1940.

the off-year Congressional elections. From 1898 to 1914, the off-year totals were 83.2 per cent of the presidential-year Congressional vote. In the five off-year elections from 1922 to 1938, inclusive, this figure shrank to 76.8 per cent. For the same two series of off-year elections, the percentages of the presidential vote were 79.3 and 70.1. Thus, in a quarter-century, the popularity of the off-year election has suffered a 10 per cent loss with the voters. If this trend continues, it may seriously affect the political position of the Congress. However, it is more probable that various interested groups will develop techniques for achieving more nearly normal support during off-years.[5]

There are obvious reasons for a party's presidential vote to be larger than its Congressional vote. In no presidential election in the modern period has the Congressional vote total equalled the total cast for the presidential electors. The Congressional figures more nearly approached those for electors in the contests of 1896, 1900, 1904, and 1908 than in any other of the thirteen presidential elections. The gap was greatest in 1932. The percentages range from 97.6 (1896 and 1900) down to 84.6 (1932).

However, in only two of the thirteen presidential elections have the Congressional totals dropped below the 90 per cent mark. Besides 1932, when one of seven who voted for F.D.R. or his opponents neglected to cast a ballot for a Congressional candidate, only 1916, with 89.1 per cent, shows a figure below the 90 per cent mark. This means, then, that generally more than ninety of every hundred voters support both presidential and Congressional candidates. The casual observer of the political scene might easily reach the conclusion that most voters are interested in presidential candidates rather than in Congressional representatives. None will deny that attention is focused upon

[5] Organizations similar to the National Political Action Committee may well perform the function of emphasizing the importance of all Congressional elections and, therefore, may popularize the off-year elections among the voters.

the national tickets, but since voters do not regard their franchise privileges as completely exercised in casting their ballots for presidential electors, doubt is certainly cast upon the accuracy of the assumption.

Straight-ticket voting may account for substantial support of the Congressional candidates. It is easy to vote for a party slate merely by putting a mark in the circle of a party-column ballot. But if that were even the dominant factor, the Congressional totals would generally follow those of the presidential votes. And this is certainly not the case. There are two important factors which operate against this easy explanation. First, a party's presidential candidate may be supported by splinter-party groups, and thus the voting strength of several groups may be united for a single presidential candidate, while the individual groups maintain their respective separate integrities in Congressional campaigns. And second, the toughness and independence of local party organization should not be underestimated in seeking the operation of general principles.

The first of these factors operated especially in 1896 and 1932. In the former year, the money issue cut across party lines with bewildering consistency. Gold Democrats supported William McKinley, and Silver Republicans, William Jennings Bryan, who was also the presidential candidate of that portion of the old Populist organization which refused to unite completely with the Democratic party. These recalcitrants nominated their own candidates for Congress and even offered their own vice-presidential candidate. Thereafter, the total Democratic Congressional percentage of its presidential vote was high until the election of 1932, when very mercurial political conditions again prevailed over the country.

The 1932 election stands apart from the other twelve in the modern period. It was the only one in which neither major party's Congressional total was within 10 per cent of its presidential vote. The figure for the Republicans was 88.8 per cent; for the Democrats it was 81.1 per cent. The country was in the trough of a deep depression. Congress was low in the public esteem. Members seeking re-election faced difficulty in framing convincing arguments in favor of their return to the House of Representatives. For the nonce, interest of the country was very definitely shifted to the presidential candidates. This phenomenon is not peculiar to the United States. The deep crisis in capitalist countries produced a more than disquieting lack of appreciation for the legislator's ability to discover the blueprints of escape from economic breakdown. In Germany, the loss of faith grew rapidly into a fuehrer-complex; in Great Britain, it moved into a parliamentary coalition with a minimum of opposition criticism; in our country, we experienced that which opposition leaders later characterized as "rubber-stamp cowardice" in our Congress. The President offered a program of "must" legislation. It mattered not that many of these bills were decidedly revolutionary in purpose; the popular demand, as interpreted by the action of the Congressional members, was that the legislative branch should not interfere with honest experimentation, even though none knew quite how the innovations would affect American political, economic, and social institutions.

In 1928, of every hundred voters, ninety-two had voted also for Congressional candidates; in 1932, that figure had dropped to slightly less than eighty-five; by 1936 it was back up again to more than ninety-four. These figures reveal the loss of esteem for the Congress and the public reliance upon the leader. Of course, there were just under three million more votes in 1932 than in 1928. Every election has its novice voters, those coming of age since the last election. Inexperience may be charged with some of the negligence, but in 1936 there were almost twice the number of new voters, of whom more than ninety-four of every hundred voted for Congressional candidates. Thus, the 1936 Congressional votes were, per hundred, over 11 per cent more than those of 1932, even though there were roughly twice as many novice voters in the later election.

The second prominent factor, which belies the theory that

the hullabaloo raised for the party's presidential ticket is instrumental in determining the preference of voters in the Congressional contests, is the prevailing and consistent toughness of local party organization. Once a party is firmly established in the local elections and has the allegiance of prominent members of the individual communities, the party will persist in strength even though the national leadership fails to compromise the inevitable differences that exist among sectional points of view. These natural antagonisms render the selection of national party nominees a matter of fine discrimination. They may destroy the availability of outstanding party leaders.

In 1944 Vice President Henry Wallace failed to secure renomination on account of his courageous stand on the Negro problem. Most Southern delegates viewed his possible renomination as an unwarranted indictment of the South. On the other hand, in the past eighty years no citizen of a Southern state, regardless of personal ability, has been nominated for the presidency by either of the two major parties. Southerners were and are unavailable; at first they were stigmatized as actually or potentially treasonable; and, since 1900, the importance of the Negro voters in the states outside the South has been such that even the national Democratic leadership could not afford to antagonize these dark-skinned voters by supporting any representative from the South for the highest office in the land. The matter of personal qualification is not involved at all, for residence in the South is for national elective office an automatic disqualification. Being practically unrepresented in the Deep South, the Republicans have nothing to gain and much to lose through nomination of a Southerner.

Sectional differences may also arise over many other political issues. Franklin D. Roosevelt was constantly embarrassed by revolts in the ranks of Southern congressmen. Being essentially an agrarian section, the South views with skepticism the measures that appear necessary to ease the tensions which persist in the industrial centers. Both of the major parties are, in truth, political coalitions, as much so as are the European coalitions against which much slipshod journalistic reporting has been directed in recent years. France, Germany, Italy, and Spain, it is urged, had unstable government on account of these coalitions. But was the Blum "left-front" any more a coalition than the pro-labor Northern and the anti-labor Southern forces which were united in the outwardly successful Rooseveltian era? If anything, the two-year term for United States House members would tend to produce greater instability of program than the longer term in France, with its practical abandonment of the use of executive dissolution of the Parliament.

The American provision for mid-term elections of House members has resulted many times in political stalemate in Washington. Any party program must, therefore, if it is to be put into operation, be completed in the first two years of a president's term, for there is danger that the party may lose control of the House and, thus, the ability to implement its program. The tragic failure of Wilson to carry out his international program derived essentially from the Republican Congressional victory of 1918. It is the duty of the opposition to oppose, and the Republicans fulfilled that responsibility admirably. My own feeling is that the situation produced an instability in world politics which prepared the way for the "blood, sweat, and tears" of recent date.

The independence of the local constituencies is traditional in the United States. The national organization is powerless to exert any very large degree of authority there. Attempts are met with charges of meddling and dictatorship. The tradition of the grass-roots is much more important to us than that of party leadership on the national level. We have a manner for keeping the leaders in their proper places. It was only a few years ago that President Roosevelt sought unsuccessfully to bring about the defeat of certain Democratic congressmen who had opposed particular portions of the New Deal program. The local constituencies displayed their independence in no uncertain terms.

Almost to a man, the anti–New Deal representatives were returned to Washington, and they returned with an undeniable mandate to oppose the entire packet of New Deal bills.

This local political integrity is further revealed in the frequent opposition to the party's presidential nominees and, at the same time, the support of the party's nominees for Congress. The election of 1904 contributes a classic example of this "scratching" of the presidential nominee. The national Democratic leadership decided that it must nominate a "gold" Democrat for the presidency, following the two defeats of Bryan. The party was a coalition, composed in part of "Silver" and "Gold" Democrats. The former had had the nominee for two elections, and the latter must be rewarded or there was danger that they might desert to the Republican camp, where belief in soft money was viewed as complete political heresy.

Judge Alton B. Parker, of New York, was nominated. The "Silver" wing deserted and voted for the popular Theodore Roosevelt, even though he was offered by the Republican opposition. But at the same time the party rank and file remained firm for the Congressional candidates. Parker received but 38 per cent of the popular votes, but Democratic congressmen got almost 42 per cent. In other words, the Congressional total constituted 105 per cent of the presidential vote, while the average percentage for the thirteen campaigns was 95. The Democratic decline over 1900 was 20 per cent in presidential and less than 13 per cent in Congressional support. Four years later the party nominated William Jennings Bryan for the third time. Then the "Gold" wing exercised its right to independence and strayed from the precincts of regularity, but the Congressional candidates were not the victims of the opposition to Bryan. Forty more Democratic congressmen than in 1904 were elected. The party's Congressional vote was 2 per cent above that for Bryan.

While the Democrats were finding it difficult to secure a national program which could satisfy their disparate groups, the Republicans were experiencing similar embarrassment. By

1910 the hidden antagonisms broke into the open in the Stalwart-Progressive controversy. The Democrats won control of the House in that year, and two years later the Republicans found themselves unable to agree upon a presidential candidate. William Howard Taft was renominated by the standpatters, while Theodore Roosevelt became the standard-bearer of the progressives or "Bull-Moose" wing. Woodrow Wilson was the Democratic nominee.

The array of three major presidential candidates produced a curious effect upon Congressional allegiances. Roosevelt drew more than half of the Republican strength, but he also lured some Democrats across to the Progressive domain. The Democratic Congressional vote was regular, and the loss in presidential support pulled Wilson's total down to approximately that of the party's Congressional candidates. Even with an increased electorate, the Wilson vote was approximately 2 per cent under Bryan's 1908 total, though the total 1912 presidential vote was 2 per cent above that of 1908.

The Republican desertion of Taft was spectacular, but the party members were much more loyal to their regular Congressional candidates. For every three supporters of Taft there were four who voted for Republican Congressional nominees. For every five who supported Roosevelt and other third-party candidates, only one voted for third-party Congressional nominees. The loss here between the national and Congressional tickets is not quite so spectacular as it appears, for many of the Republican Congressional candidates, such as George Norris, of Nebraska, were supporting Roosevelt. Thus, votes for such candidates were, in reality, for the progressive rather than for the regular standpat wing.

In the thirteen presidential elections, the major parties' Congressional votes varied from 65.1 per cent to 135.2 per cent of the presidential total.[6] Herbert Hoover ran farthest ahead of his Congressional candidates, as they received but 65 per cent of

[6] Only Republican and Democratic votes are included in this analysis.

his vote. Much of this scratching came in the South where dry and anti-Catholic candidates for Congress gave to the Democrats the opportunity for remaining regular with part of their ticket. As proof of this, Mr. Hoover received a million votes more than Mr. Coolidge had polled four years earlier in that section.[7] Mr. Hoover was, in addition, extremely popular in other sections, regardless of his stand on prohibition. He was an engineer, with the "know-how" in the scientific world. Was it not possible that this exponent of applied science could utilize the scientific techniques to abolish poverty and the necessity for public charity?

The nadir of all major presidential-candidate popularity, in terms of the Congressional vote, was William Howard Taft in 1912. Of course, the Republicans were split into the two warring camps. Many of the states had Bull-Moose (Progressive) Congressional tickets, and support for them reduced substantially the total Republican Congressional vote. In fact, the Republican presidential vote of 1908 was more than twice that which Taft received in 1912, and 163 per cent of the vote which Republican Congressional candidates received in the same election. The difference between 163 and 135 (Congressional percentage of 1912 presidential vote) reveals approximately the support for the Progressive Congressional candidates. It proves also the tenacity of local party organization. The Roosevelt Progressives experienced much greater difficulty in taking over local party organization than in finding support for presidential, senatorial, and gubernatorial candidates.

A fairly reliable criterion of presidential-candidate popularity may be secured through the establishment of the normal position of the head of the major-party ticket in relation to the

[7] The Coolidge Southern vote was 933,100, while that for Hoover was 1,993,583, a gain of 113.6 per cent. On the other hand, the Southern Republican votes for congressmen increased only from 678,114 to 1,006,321, or 48.4 per cent increase over the 1924 total. Thus the increase for Hoover was three and one-quarter times that of the Republican increase in Southern Congressional votes.

support received by the party's Congressional candidates in their particular constituencies. In the thirteen presidential campaigns of the modern era, the political fortunes of the twenty-six presidential candidates of the major parties reveal the wide variation noted above. The mean between the high of 65.1 per cent (Hoover, 1928) and the low of 135.2 per cent (Taft, 1912) was 93.9 per cent.[8] Ostensibly, the highs and the lows are the products of special and peculiar conditions, such as party schisms, multiple party support of a single candidate, and so on. Thus the normal relationship between presidential and Congressional support is not the average of the twenty-six percentages. Accordingly, the five highs and five lows have been eliminated from the list. The remaining sixteen percentages represent the more permanent and substantial aspects of the party battle. These sixteen extend from 88.8 per cent (Hoover, 1932) to 99 per cent (Wilson, 1912); the mean of the sixteen is 93.9 per cent.

Using this rigged mean as the criterion, the record of the twenty-six major party candidacies is, in order of efficiency, as follows:[9]

1. H. Hoover, Republican, 1928.
2. F. D. Roosevelt, Democrat, 1932.
3. W. Wilson, Democrat, 1916.
4. F. D. Roosevelt, Democrat, 1936.
5. W. J. Bryan, Democrat, 1896.
6. H. Hoover, Republican, 1932.
7. W. G. Harding, Republican, 1920.
8. F. D. Roosevelt, Democrat, 1940.
9. T. Roosevelt, Republican, 1904.
10. F. D. Roosevelt, Democrat, 1944.
11. W. H. Taft, Republican, 1908.

[8] The individual percentages for each of the parties in each of the elections are shown on page 19.
[9] The efficiency of the presidential ticket in relation to the normal average of Congressional vote was for both parties in the thirteen elections, as shown on page 19.

12. C. E. Hughes, Republican, 1916.
13. C. C. Coolidge, Republican, 1924.
14. W. B. McKinley, Republican, 1896.
15. W. B. McKinley, Republican, 1900.
16. W. Willkie, Republican, 1940.
17. W. J. Bryan, Democrat, 1900.
18. A. E. Smith, Democrat, 1928.
19. T. E. Dewey, Republican, 1944.
20. W. Wilson, Democrat, 1912.
21. J. Cox, Democrat, 1920.
22. W. J. Bryan, Democrat, 1908.
23. A. Landon, Republican, 1936.
24. A. Parker, Democrat, 1904.
25. J. W. Davis, Democrat, 1924.
26. W. H. Taft, Republican, 1912.

In the upper ten of these major-party presidential candidacies, the Democrats had seven and the Republicans three. All four of the F. D. Roosevelt races were included, which reveals again the popularity which he enjoyed from citizens who did not vote for Democratic Congressional candidates. Only one (Hoover, 1932) failed to win his race. The answer here is that the Republican Congressional vote fell off sharply. In the lowest ten candidacies, there were seven Democrats and three Republicans. Of these ten, only one (Wilson, 1912) was elected. This apparent contradiction came about through the Republican schism of 1912. In the middle sixteen, the ones who established the criterion, there were six Democrats and ten Republicans, which means that the Republicans have been a more consistent party. They have displayed better leadership in that they have co-ordinated their Congressional and national tickets and have voted their rank and file with more regularity. The Democrats were plagued with factionalism, both in the early period, when the Populist wing went all out for bimetallism, and in the later period, when F. D. Roosevelt built his coalition among the farmers, labor, and the traditional Democrats of the South. Without F.D.R.'s leadership, the Democrats have a decidedly inferior efficiency record as contrasted with the Republicans, for the nine elections from 1896 to 1928 show a Democratic efficiency rating of 95.6 per cent. During the same period the Republican national ticket compiled a remarkable record of 102.6 per cent, and, omitting the schism of 1912, the Republican mark was 106.8 per cent.

There are obvious reasons for the consistency of the Republican record. The party is not so nationally universal as the Democratic party. Republican victories are achieved in the East, the Middle West, and the West, with occasional assistance from the Border states. The Democrats exist as a going organization in all sections. This accounts for the fact that an F. D. Roosevelt landslide secured a larger percentage of the electoral vote than a greater popular landslide by Herbert Hoover. The "solid South" continues its eighty-year-old policy of voting Democratic. Some authorities have characterized the Republicans as being a "sectional party." This designation is not overly important, for the success of the "sectional party" belies the inference behind it. Not since its inception has this party been reduced to the status in which it was neither the government nor the opposition, for its organic strength in three-fourths of the forty-eight states makes it a persistent contender for political supremacy. Moreover, during the fifty years covered in this study, conditions had to be peculiarly favorable in the non-Southern sections to make possible a Democratic victory.

The story of presidential ticket efficiency for the two major parties is depicted in Graph III. In only two elections, 1916 and 1932, were both party national tickets above the 100 per cent line. And both of these were dramatic elections, in which little voting strength was commanded by third-party presidential candidates. The European war furnished the backdrop for the first, and the race was fought over the official policy which this country should adopt in that dramatic situation. The generally

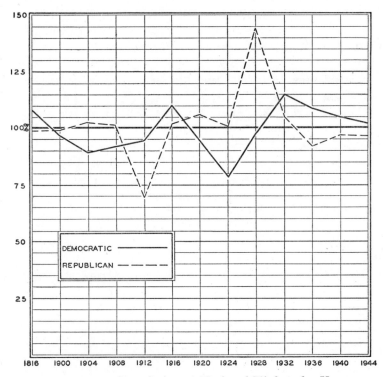

GRAPH III : *Popularity of National Tickets by Years*

pacifist convictions of the country returned Wilson to power on his record of "He kept us out of war." In 1932 the domestic scene furnished the principal motives for that epoch-making election. The momentum of the Republicans was slowed by "Black Friday" and its aftermath. The habit of voting Republican was not enough to dissipate the optimism for Mr. Roosevelt's avowed assistance to "the forgotten man." It matters not that some of "the barefoot boys from Wall Street"—as Mr. Ickes, the self-styled curmudgeon of the New Deal, labeled them— thought that they could qualify for admission into the select circle of forgotten men. The idea had tremendous popular appeal. Laborers, farmers, white-collar workers, and small-business men joined the throng, and the sanctity of the Republican shibboleth—"The Democrats are bad for business"—was successfully challenged. Again, no strong third-party candidates bid for presidential votes, and the suffrage was divided between Mr. Roosevelt and Mr. Hoover.

For the period, seven Republican and six Democratic candidates are above the line, and seven Democrats and six Republicans below it. The Democrats won but one election (1912) with less than a 100 per cent mark, while the Republicans won two (1896 and 1900). Also the Democrats lost but one (1896) when above the mark, while the Republicans lost two (1916 and 1932). Thus, to insure victory, it is safer for a candidate to run ahead of the Congressional candidates of his party, although this alone will not insure success; for of the thirteen candidates who exceeded the criterion established, only ten were elected, and of the thirteen who failed to achieve it, three were elected to the presidency.

The Battle in the Constituencies

THE election of congressmen is not comparable to that of the president. At least, the president seeks his office upon the basis of a policy or program. It may be ill defined, general, or ambiguous, but it nevertheless reflects the nominee's personal convictions or his appreciation of the demands of political expediency. This is not so with Congressional candidates. In the same party, candidates will support policies which together run the full gamut of the ideological scale. Thus, some Democrats seek the office upon an unadulterated program of denying the suffrage to Negroes; and other Democrats will ask election upon a promise to remove all racial barriers to political participation. Likewise, there will be free-trade Republicans, and high-tariff Republicans; pro-social-security Democrats and anti-social-security Democrats; nationalistic Socialists and internationalists of the same political designation.

As a result, the members of a Congressional party have little to bind them together except the questionable desire to govern or to oppose the national administration. At least, for purposes of Congressional organization, they will find their individual ways into the party caucuses.

We are not interested here in the campaign promises of candidates. We may make the assumption, faulty though it is, that candidates will generally propose policies which are viewed kindly by the popular majorities in their constituencies. Of course, there may indeed be some candidates who are sufficiently high-principled to advocate policies which are foredoomed to defeat. A candidate of this kind is, of course, of great value in representative democracy, and should rightly be considered as contributing as much to our government as his opponent who is elected and placed upon the public pay roll. Is it any more reasonable that the public should pay the winner than the loser? Indeed, it may be compensating a spineless nincompoop while it neglects an intelligent citizen who has contributed the means by which the constituency could make its decision. It is only another illustration of the American adage, "Nothing succeeds like success." But it tends to breed a kind of politics which abstains whenever possible from facing the issues and which makes our political campaigns into contests in which there is "much ado about nothing." As a group, the candidates of the splinter parties, such as Socialist and Prohibition, are the only ones who create their own issues and give their all to the education of the electorate and to the greater clarification of issues. However, if one of these splinter groups were to become one of the major parties, its candidates would, in order to achieve success, have to adopt the chameleonism of traditional politics.

The Constitution provides for election of representatives from districts whose boundaries are determined by state legislatures. That the "fathers" did not visualize the manner and results of party development in this country is beside the point. They hoped evidently that the majority views of the local districts would, through the inevitable necessity for compromise, be able to formulate a national program. The liberty of the individual would be protected under such a system, for the representatives would scarcely be expected to support bills which promised to injure their localities. This was the philosophy of agrarian America during the era of the Revolution. Tyranny originated in government or in the church. The potential victims were placed, therefore, in positions of power. Insufficient emphasis has been given to this fundamental factor in the origin of political democracy.

If the "fathers" had visualized political-party development, they might well have provided a system which would have produced a general program for all the party's official Congressional candidates. The list system, implemented by several European states, represents such constitutional recognition of the primary role of political parties. The parties themselves choose their own parliamentary representatives, and the choice presumably is made upon the basis of regularity and individual ability. However, authority of this nature leads, and it did in Europe, to institutionalism of the party system, to an inner aristocracy of control, and to ostentatious neglect of the public welfare. Under a system such as this, the party program is the important thing. Too much attention is given in the legislative bodies to political scholasticism, to statement and restatement of the great party principles, even though the program was presumably formulated as a guide to political action and not as a substitute for it.

In the twenty-five Congressional elections analyzed here, 10,148 seats were filled by selection from individual-member districts. In addition, 255 members were chosen in at-large elections.[1] The at-large method of selection gives a concession to parties and reduces the influence of the local community. But there is no apparent demand for its substitution in place of the Constitutional provision. In fact, it is utilized primarily as an aid to state legislatures in meeting the difficulties inherent in redistricting their states. With the rules now in force limiting the legislatures, it becomes difficult, or even impossible in many cases, to achieve a division of a state into districts without patent

[1] This means that 2½ per cent were elected at large. The record is spotted. In fact, two elections (1912 and 1932) contributed eighty-one (31.76 per cent) of these at-large congressmen, for the apparent reason that the state legislatures were either dilatory or constitutionally inept in redistricting their states. The percentage records for the first four decades of this century show at-large congressmen to be, respectively, 2.5, 3, 0.5 and 4.4. This means that the twenties, the only decade in which there was no reapportionment of the lower house, were the most settled decade politically. However, it should be remarked that the first congresses after reapportionments have larger numbers of at-large congressmen. As the twenties had no reapportionment, the small number of at-large congressmen, therefore, has a reasonable basis.

inequities, to say nothing of the political penalties that may be involved.[2]

In the twenty-five elections, 4,349 Republican candidates received more than 50 per cent of the votes in their individual contests. This mark of 42.9 per cent was exceeded by the Democrats with 47.1 per cent.[3] Yet it must be remembered that the Republicans were the majority party in thirteen of the twenty-five Congresses. A breakdown of these majority decisions is shown in Graph IV. Here is the real story in Congressional elections. The majority decision is the back-log of every Congress. The Republicans led in thirteen, the Democrats in twelve. Only in 1930 was this criterion not an accurate index of the party winner; the Democrats led by one percentage point, even though the Republicans elected one more congressman in the single-member contests.[4] That the Democrats were, through the deaths of Republican congressmen-elect, able to organize the House could not under any stretch of the imagination be attributed to the higher percentage figure of that party, unless the analyst were simply seeking to attribute causation to mere coincidence.

The graph reveals the basic trends in a half-century of American politics. The terrific nosedive of the Republicans in the second decade of the present century had its origin in internal Republican party struggle. But it was a temporary phenomenon and did not substantially improve the Democratic majority-decision percentages. As the minority party in the quartet of elections (1902 to 1908) before the break in Republi-

[2] From 1840 to 1930, the reapportionment acts of Congress have specifically provided for districts of contiguous territory. In later ones, the rule of compactness was added. The last two acts have not included these qualifications, and the Supreme Court has said that the omission was not to be construed as merely accidental. See *Wood* v. *Broom*, 287 U. S. 1 (1932).

[3] The Democrats elected 4,775 members by a majority vote.

[4] The percentage points were 49.4 (Democratic) and 48.3 (Republican), but of the 433 single-member contests, the Republicans won 216, the Democrats 215, and third parties 2. In addition, 2 Republicans were elected at large.

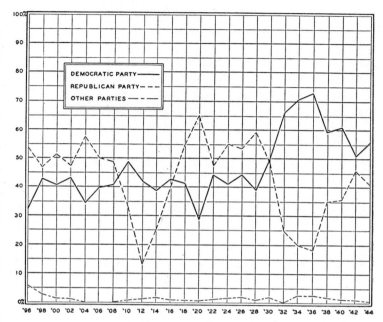

GRAPH IV : *Percentage of Seats Won by Majority Vote by Parties and Years*

can control, the Democratic average was 39.4 per cent; as the majority party in the next four, the average rose only to 42.5 per cent; and as the minority party in the next four elections (1918 to 1924), the average fell to 38.9 per cent. Similar averages for the Republicans show percentages of 50.9, 27.9, and 55.2. The obvious explanation of these figures is that, as parties were organized and as issues were fought, there were simply more Republicans in the country. Only their failure to agree upon a program and leadership permitted the Democrats to come to power.

The same explanation cannot be made for the political break that came in 1930. The Republicans slid down the political scale, not because of internecine strife but through the creation of positive favor for the Democratic program. Since 1930 the Republican graph-line behaves much more like the line of a minority party. It pulled out of the trough of the three elections from 1932 to 1936, but it showed no tendency to challenge successfully the majority-party figures. Even the election of 1942 was more the result of special conditions than of a resuscitation of Republican popularity. The millions of workers and soldiers, busy in the war effort, found themselves unable to vote for congressmen. And the 1944 Republican decline was a serious blow to the party's future, for after three elections in which it improved upon the one immediately preceding, the opportunity was present for the party to come to power if the prior trends had been built upon fundamental citizens attitudes.

The discussion above is not an attempt to prophesy a brilliant future of continued success for the Democrats. The Democratic coalition of labor, farmer, and minority peoples' support was essentially the triumph of the political skill of Franklin Delano Roosevelt. And the party may indeed find it difficult to keep the team working in unison toward Democratic success. Even now the basic ideological difficulties manifest in the traditional Southern congressmen's opposition to the program of the Northern liberals presages the end of an era unless the Southerners forego their announced convictions or the Republicans continue to stand adamant against any pronounced liberalization of program. Thus the New Deal electoral successes were not alone the product of skillful leadership; many of them had their foundations in the sheer stupidity of the Republican opposition, which had, probably unknown to itself, lost contact with the vital opinion in the country. Through four presidential campaigns, the Republicans continued to return to the slogans with which they had won fifty years before. If they move to a position left of center, there is little doubt that Democratic hegemony could end very quickly, for the Southern congressmen are indeed a heavy burden upon the dominant Northern and Western liberalism.

54

In only six of the twenty-five elections were less than 90 per cent of the congressmen chosen by majority vote, those from 1906 through 1916. The chief factor again was the split in the Republican party, though the Socialist and Prohibition splinters were in some parts of the country commanding sufficient popular strength to disturb the normal functioning of the two-party system. The influence of third parties will be considered later in this study, but it is appropriate here to observe that our Congressional elections have featured especially the battle between two major parties.

Of the more than ten thousand congressmen elected in single-member constituencies, over 91 per cent were chosen by majority as against mere plurality decision. The high was in 1944, when 425 of the 426 congressmen were the majority choices of their constituencies. The low was in 1912, when only 55.7 per cent were similarly selected. Of course, the twenties were collectively the most consistent of the period, for of the more than two thousand representatives chosen, just under 97 per cent were selected by majority decision. The disintegration of the Republicans in the election on 1932 dropped the figure to 92 per cent, but in each of the six contests thereafter, the percentage is increased over that of its immediate predecessor until the climax of 1944, when only one congressman failed to secure a majority.

NUMBER OF SEATS CONTESTED

In the spread of party strength, there is a distinct difference between the two great parties. Being so predominantly Democratic, the South is, in itself, a reason for the fact that the Republicans each year contest far fewer seats than their Democratic rivals.[5] As an example, in 1942 the Republicans nominated no candidates in 82 of the South's 112 districts, and in four

[5] The number of seats in which the parties received less than one-half of 1 per cent of the vote, and the percentages, are shown on page 57.

others their candidates were evidently of the most nominal character, for none of them received as much as one-half of 1 per cent of the poll. The war year of 1918 presents almost the same picture with 82 seats uncontested by the Republicans and 2 others in the excessive futility class.

The decline in generality of Republican strength has increased from an average of 10.2 per cent in the first five elections (1896–1904) to 18.4 per cent in the last five (1936–44). This means that that party is now contesting some thirty-five fewer seats than it would have contested under the earlier ratio. Naturally, with fewer contests, the Republicans must win a larger percentage of the others in order to secure majority control of the House; for instance, to secure a majority in 1942, the Republicans would have had to win 65 per cent of the seats which they contested; in 1944, the necessary majority could have been achieved with 60 per cent of their contested seats. As this percentage increases, the task of the party leaders becomes more difficult.

On the other hand, the Democrats have maintained a very consistent record, presenting a noncontesting average of only 2.9 per cent for the first decade and one of 2.4 per cent in the last five elections. Their lowest era was in the twenties, as for the seven elections from 1918–30 their average rose to 7.5 per cent. However, for the twenty-five elections, their figure of 398 (or 3.9 per cent) contrasts emphatically with the Republicans' 1,540 (or 15.2 per cent). Thus the Democrats have rarely to win more than 52 per cent of their contests in order to secure majority control of the House.[6]

[6] This feature of the party clash is important only in the contests in which 10 per cent of the vote was secured, for vote totals under that figure scarcely represent a threat to the other party. The percentages of their contests above the 10 per cent level, necessary to majority control, the percentage of such contests actually won, and the percentages of the necessary majority won, were for each of the elections as shown on page 57.

Note 5, page 55.

PERCENTAGE RECEIVING LESS THAN 0.5 PER CENT VOTE

No.	1896	98	1900	02	04	06	08	10	12	14	16	18	20	22	24	26	28	30	32	34	36	38	40	42	44	Total
Republican	28	40	27	50	40	38	50	8	6	8	10	42	61	56	66	56	83	61	94	63	85	77	96	69		1540
Democrat	17	9	7	12	6	17	5	8	6	10	41	31	28	26	42	18	41	9	7	10	12	8	12	8		398
Others	91	95	93	108	104	98	124	143	74	53	108	213	179	237	245	287	274	280	171	166	168	243	272	322	329	4477

%	1896	98	1900	02	04	06	08	10	12	14	16	18	20	22	24	26	28	30	32	34	36	38	40	42	44
Rep.	8.0	11.4	7.7	13.3	10.6	13.3	9.9	15.8	20.8	19.0	10.4	21.0	9.8	14.1	13.0	15.2	12.7	19.2	16.0	22.2	14.8	20.0	18.1	22.7	16.2
Dem.	4.9	2.6	2.0	3.2	1.6	4.5	1.3	2.1	1.5	1.9	2.4	9.6	7.2	6.5	6.1	9.7	4.2	9.5	2.4	1.7	1.7	2.8	1.9	2.8	1.9

Note 6, page 56.

PERCENTAGE OF SEATS ABOVE 10 PER CENT NECESSARY FOR MAJORITY CONTROL

	1896	98	1900	02	04	06	08	10	12	14	16	18	20	22	24	26	28	30	32	34	36	38	40	42	44
Rep.	56.1	58.0	55.5	58.5	57.4	59.6	56.6	60.3	65.5	62.4	58.8	63.8	56.7	61.0	59.1	61.3	58.8	63.2	62.1	64.5	60.9	63.4	62.1	65.2	61.7
Dem.	52.9	51.8	51.3	52.1	51.2	52.5	50.8	52.2	51.0	51.2	51.2	55.6	54.8	53.7	54.1	54.7	52.5	55.8	51.3	51.1	51.3	51.9	51.2	52.1	51.3

PERCENTAGE OF SEATS ABOVE 10 PER CENT WON BY EACH PARTY

	1896	98	1900	02	04	06	08	10	12	14	16	18	20	22	24	26	28	30	32	34	36	38	40	42	44
Rep.	66.4	62.1	62.8	64.2	75.5	69.7	64.6	53.1	45.1	57.7	59.1	73.6	79.5	64.4	69.5	70.7	74.6	65.7	37.6	31.2	26.9	50.1	47.1	63.6	56.5
Dem.	39.4	47.6	45.0	49.6	38.2	46.5	46.2	60.3	69.5	55.5	51.5	47.3	36.5	53.2	49.3	51.9	41.0	55.7	73.3	76.3	79.1	63.5	64.4	53.2	56.4

PERCENTAGE OF NECESSARY MAJORITY PERCENTAGE WHICH EACH PARTY WON

	1896	98	1900	02	04	06	08	10	12	14	16	18	20	22	24	26	28	30	32	34	36	38	40	42	44
Rep.	118.4	107.0	113.2	109.8	131.5	117.0	114.1	88.1	68.9	92.5	100.5	115.4	140.2	105.6	117.6	115.3	126.9	104.5	60.5	48.2	44.2	79.0	75.8	97.5	91.6
Dem.	74.5	91.9	87.7	95.2	74.6	88.6	90.9	115.5	136.3	108.4	100.6	85.1	58.0	99.1	78.9	94.9	78.1	99.9	142.9	149.3	154.2	122.4	125.8	102.1	109.9

PERCENTAGE DISTRIBUTION OF PARTY STRENGTH

The continuous Democratic complexion of the South naturally affects the distribution of party strength. In the entire country, of the seats won with percentages from 75 to 100, the Democrats have secured 81.3 per cent. Thus for every Republican there are four Democratic congressmen in that category. The effect upon the opposite end of the percentage gamut is equally decisive. Of the 2,149 races in which a major party received less than 10 per cent of the vote, the Republicans account for 1,710 (79.6 per cent) and the Democrats but 439 (20.4 per cent). These facts reveal that the Republican strength lies for the most part in the middle categories, especially in the classes from 30 to 60 per cent. Thus they led the Democrats in

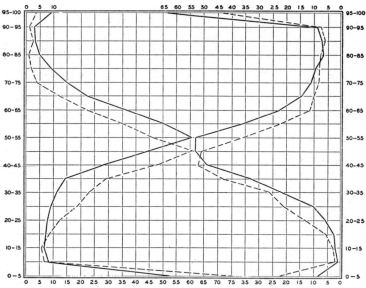

GRAPH V : *Average Party Record by Percentage Categories*

Republican   Democrat
Majority elections——   Majority elections——
Minority elections----   Minority elections----

the 50 to 75 per cent category 3,881 to 2,734 (58.7 per cent to 41.3 per cent). The Democrats must, therefore, lead in the brackets from 25 to 50.[7]

The vagaries of these percentage behaviors are interesting. In the fourteen Republican victories, their figures in the 50-to-55 category were without exception larger than those in the 45-to-50 group. On the other hand, the Democratic numbers in the latter category have exceeded those in the first in six of their eleven victories. If the Democrats succeed in reversing this arrangement, they achieve pronounced sweeps in the election, as they did from 1932 to 1940, inclusive. This means, too, that the Democratic minority is consistently larger than the Republican, even in the years of greatest adversity. The safe seats in the South account for this fact.[8]

The peculiarities in the distribution of party strength are succinctly revealed in Graph V. The average distribution is shown for each party in its winning and losing elections.[9] Of course, the graph is not a picture of any two elections, one a Republican and one a Democratic triumph. Rather it is a composite picture, and if there have been pronounced trends in the last fifty years of American politics, these trends are revealed only in the common averages.

For the Republicans, the concentration of power in the middle-percentage categories is the conspicuous rule. Even when they lose, they place a very large number of candidates in the almost-won column of between 45 and 50 per cent. Their two most numerous categories are the almost-won (45 to 50 per cent) and the barely-won (from 50 to 55 per cent). Their average of only 27 congressmen in the bracket from 75 to 100 per

[7] Of the 7,987 in this category, the Democrats had 4,504 (56.4 per cent) and the Republicans 3,483 (43.6 per cent).

[8] The lowest Democratic numbers were in 1896 (130) and in 1920 (136), while the Republicans secured but 88 in 1936, 99 in 1934, and 109 in 1932.

[9] The Republicans won majorities or pluralities in fourteen elections, the Democrats in eleven.

cent contrasts strongly with the Democratic figure of 73. Thus, when the Republicans win, they must pick up somewhere in the neighborhood of 190 seats from the contests in which they secure only from one-half to three-fourths of the votes, or from the three-cornered races which are featured in a few constituencies.

Likewise, in winning elections the 5 to 40 per cent categories comprise only sixty-three Republican losses, which means that, not counting the fifty-one which they do not contest, in almost 84 per cent of their races they achieve the distinction of securing more than 40 per cent of the votes. This means, then, considering the probable presence of third parties, that any one of those 284 contests in which they poll more than 40 per cent of the votes, there is the possibility of winning a Congressional post. The three categories in which the Republican increase is greatest in their losing over their winning elections are those from twenty-five to forty per cent. Each of them more than doubles the winning-year figures. Likewise, the categories from 70 to 85 per cent increase most in their winning years.

The Democratic strength has been more general throughout the United States. Even before the formation of the Roosevelt coalition in 1932, it was to be found in every section. But in states without slaveholding traditions, the Democrats were, except on rare occasions, the minority party. The growth of organized labor and its departure from the old Gompers neutrality policy has altered the political complexion of many industrial states. Of course, when a section regularly contributes a hundred congressmen to a party, that party is in an enviable position, for those hundred seats become a veritable backlog, to which may be added seats here and there from pockets of strength in the Republican states.

In the average for their winning elections, almost 68 per cent of the Democratic congressmen received more than 60 per cent of the votes in their contests. As pointed out above, this contrasts distinctly with the Republican data. Also, the spread of

Democratic strength in the middle categories is wider than, if not quite so deep, that of the Republicans. Even in winning years, the Democrats have more candidates in the group from 45 to 50 per cent than in that from 50 to 55 per cent. Thus, if the surge of Democratic popularity is sufficient to push the erstwhile 40 per cent constituencies into the majority class, the victory assumes landslide proportions. This happened first in 1932, and was repeated in four elections immediately following. All were Democratic sweeps. In the last two elections (1942 and 1944), the increase of Republican popularity forced more Democratic candidates into the category immediately below the majority mark. Yet the soundness of Democratic organization kept its candidates from falling into the brackets below 30 per cent, for of the 426 races in 1944, only fifteen (3.5 per cent) constituencies gave official Democratic candidates less than 30 per cent of their suffrage. In the entire fifty-year period, the Republicans have never experienced such general popularity.

Third Parties and Splinters

IT is not easy to appraise the influence which third parties have exerted upon Congressional elections. Splinter parties are as much a part of the American political scene as is the general non-ideological character of our two major parties. Third parties may fall into several groups. They may result from internecine strife in one of the major parties. The Progressives of 1912 illustrate this type of political offshoot. The struggle for supremacy within the erstwhile organization proceeds all the way down from the national committee to the lowliest precincts. In 1912 local leaders had generally "to stand up and be counted," either as Taft or "T.R." men. Naturally a schism, which features a line of cleavage somewhere near the middle of the total membership will achieve phenomenal results in popular support. In the last half-century, the Progressives of 1912 were the strongest third party of our political history, though it should be noted that their success in the Congressional field was not so spectacular as was the support which Theodore Roosevelt received as presidential candidate.

The LaFollette Progressives of 1924 were similar to their cousins of 1912, for they comprised the liberal wing of the Republican party. The liberals were seeking to chastize the conservatives. Principal differences arose in regard to governmental intervention in economic affairs. The attempt of 1924 proved to be more sectional in its aspects than the break of twelve years before. Only Wisconsin, Minnesota, and several states in the West gave strong support to the LaFollette party. There were several reasons for this failure. Scant attention was devoted to local party organization. The LaFollette group was handicapped in that it had very little money with which to organize the constituencies. Most of its attention went to the presidential race and to specific gubernatorial and senatorial candidacies. Magnificent though he had been during a long and energetic career in state and national politics, the elder LaFollette was in nowise so spectacular a public figure as T.R. His reputation was the product of day-by-day struggle for liberalism. He was unmistakably sound in his approach, from the liberal point of view. But presidential candidates must, if not favored by strong local organization, establish their prestige through spectacular personal appeal to voters, and Senator LaFollette was not by nature endowed with the indescribable qualities which go to produce political "It." Like Henry Clay, he could through almost interminable speeches establish to the immediate satisfaction of his hearers the accuracy of his contentions, but unlike Andrew Jackson he did not have the capacity to compel followers to vote for him without apparent reason. And withal, most voters are inclined to support candidates on emotional rather than sheerly intellectual grounds.

There was another factor in the failure of the LaFollette Progressives to establish themselves as an alternative to both the Republicans and the Democrats. The liberal drive of 1912 had failed. The party leaders who had remained loyal in that crisis were rewarded in the years which followed, and many promising leaders were penalized for having been irregular. Institutions generally put much greater emphasis upon loyalty than upon intellectual acumen. Persons who become the leaders of tomorrow must be broken to the traces today. This is a rule of any institutional hierarchy, and men with aspirations for institutional careers learn soon the necessity for regularity. Many prominent Republicans who may well have personally preferred LaFollette to Coolidge in 1924 were, consciously or otherwise, deterred from acting upon their personal preferences. As the very astute Thomas Marshall is supposed to have remarked to a delegation of ministers who came to enlist his official aid, as governor, in the cause of liquor prohibition: "Gentlemen, you don't actually believe that I could permit my religious and moral scruples to stand in the way of my political advancement!" Thus, but for the precedent of 1912, the LaFollette revolt might have assumed greater political proportions.

The two Progressive rebellions against the Republican party contributed considerable confusion to the pattern of American politics, for they offered a second alternative to the majority party. The same, but with less optimism for success, applied to the Populists. They surged to the top in a few agricultural states in 1890 and 1892. Official fusion with the Democrats in 1896 did not terminate the revolt. For a dozen years there were traces of this agrarian protest in the official returns of the elections. Some of the Populists refused to join the Democrats. To them, it was a "plague on both your houses." In its inception, the Populist movement was more of a threat to the Democrats than to the Republicans. Local Democratic organizations were taken over by the revolters in several states; in others, candidates for a fusion (Democratic-Populist) ticket battled the Republicans in the Congressional campaigns. Some of the Congressional impotency of the Democrats from 1896 to 1910 derived from the party's inability to bring the disparate anti-administration groups into the Democratic fold. Indeed, it is not at all improbable that, if greater cleverness had abided in the leadership of the party, the Democrats might have enjoyed a rather extended tenure in national office following the election of Cleveland in 1884. The Republicans had, in taking the responsibilities of the governing party, created a cumulative popular majority against them. But the Democrats, and especially those from the Southern states, preferred purity of principle (as they saw it) to popular support. As a result, the party was deprived of the advantages accruing from the loss of popular respect for the Republicans.

The Progressive and Populist movements originated in intra-party disharmony, but by far most third-party candidacies came from splinter groups, whose programs envisaged revolutionary changes in the United States. The Socialist and Socialist Labor parties are illustrative of these splinter groups. None would maintain, least of all their members, that they were sanguinary concerning chances for immediate success. Rather, they were primarily engaged in a program of education, of the creation of new perspectives upon particular problems of social importance, and of the ultimate coming to power when the new political atmosphere would create that possibility. These political sects were, therefore, ideological. They sought to create opinion, rather than merely to put their ears to the ground and listen intently for the first faint murmurings of the still, small voice of the populace. It is impossible to measure their success in the educational field. Whatever it may have been, splinter parties are fated to remain in that category or undergo the embarrassment of being swallowed by one or the other, or both, of the great parties; for whenever a splinter party popularizes an idea with the voters, the swallowing ordeal is on the agenda for quick consummation. There exists no way in which monopoly rights may be achieved in the field of political ideas. Many newspapers and commentators "on the right" never tired of reminding the American public that President Franklin Roosevelt's New Deal had adopted many planks from the Socialist platform. But if the reminder was intended to discredit the Democrats, which was its patent purpose, there is no evidence of its success. Rather, the charge probably did no more than to emphasize the opportunism of the New Deal and, therefore, to strengthen its support from the common man.

A third variety of minor parties comprises those of local character. The Progressives of Wisconsin, the Farmer-Laborites of Minnesota, and the American Labor party members of New York represent this grouping. The first two became the major parties of their respective states. In both, the Democratic membership was so insignificant as to represent no threat to continuous Republican hegemony. A split in Republican ranks produced an effective alternative, and the alternative, appealing to Democrats, Socialists, and disaffected agrarians, grew into the major-party status. Governors were elected and congressmen sent to Washington. When fissures of this nature occur in the dominant party, there is likelihood of creating a three-party system which, under normal conditions, causes minority government. This situation might well have developed in the South except for the disfranchisement of so many potential electors. From 1932 to 1944 there were 110 congressmen elected in three-party contests in which none of the winners received a majority of the votes cast. Interestingly enough, 49 (41.2 per cent) were from the Middle West, and 47 of these 49 were from Wisconsin and Minnesota.[1]

Third parties perform an entirely wholesome function in our political system. They are, as Woodrow Wilson once said relative to the newer instruments of direct democracy, "the rusty gun behind the door." When the two major parties perform their respective functions of government and opposition, the need for third parties, except as political educational agencies for the refinement of future issues, scarcely exists. But the mere persistence of these splinters creates a continuing atmosphere in which the two major parties are unable to crystallize any preponderant opinion for sacerdotalism. Thus, the purity of the non-ideological character of our party system is maintained largely through the threat of third parties. At least, a splinter has the potential right to replace one of the major parties, and that threat is sufficient to prevent bipartisan conspiracy to neglect the public welfare. The major parties must practice alertness or face the possibility that the rusty gun will be dragged from its place of concealment.

There are various estimates on the influence which third parties have exerted upon our political history. There is no place here to attempt an appraisal of their success in the education of

[1] Twenty-five were from Wisconsin and twenty-two from Minnesota. The figure for the latter would undoubtedly have been larger but for the fact that all Minnesota congressmen were elected at-large in 1932.

66

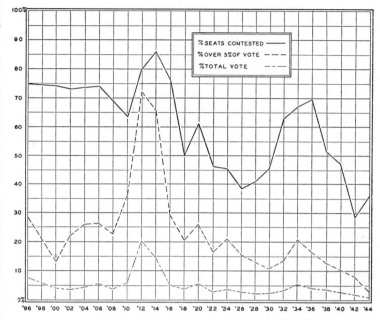

GRAPH VI : *Third Party Percentages by Years*

the electorate. Major parties have, on many occasions, adopted platform principles which were first proposed by minor parties. The "noble experiment" of prohibition sprang from such a low-ly origin. On the other hand, we may measure, in part, the effect which third-party candidacies have had upon the numerical results of an election.

The factual story of third parties is depicted in Graph VI. The first generalization from the graph is that third parties are becoming less important in the selection of congressmen.[2] In only two elections (1912 and 1914) have they polled more than

[2] Their average popular vote for the period of 1896 to 1916, featured by Populist, Progressive, and Socialist campaigns, was 7.4 per cent; but during the past twenty-eight years the average has fallen to 3.4 per cent. In 1944, it was less than 1 per cent.

67

7.5 per cent of the total vote. In the twenty-five elections, they averaged only 4.5 per cent. This does not mean that third parties may not have been important in some elections and in some states; but it is obvious that the overall influence has not been great.

There are patent reasons for this decline in strength. In the period following the Civil War, the Republicans were in unbroken control of the government for twenty years. As always happens, the responsibility of governing alienated many erstwhile Republicans from the party. They joined agricultural protest movements or the Democratic opposition. Grover Cleveland, a Democrat, was elected president, but there was no appreciable liberalization of legislative program. Many persons turned to the Populist movement, when they could support neither major party. Some voters had been members of both in the years before. Official fusion with the Democrats in 1896 apparently placated most of the Populists, but many remained die-hard oppositionists. However, they found some relief in the Wilson administrations. The rapidly maturing industrial order and the rush to urban centers created an urgency in our politics which had not been there before. An agrarian order may absorb economic shocks with greater equanimity than an urban society. Since 1918, even with the revolt of the LaFollette Progressives and the Farmer Laborites, the popularity of third parties has appreciably diminished. To support a candidate who is certain of defeat may be enough where sheer spitefulness is the purpose, but it will scarcely satisfy the conscience of a worker, a farmer, or a merchant who feels that one of the major parties is definitely antithetical to his interests. Therefore, it is more reasonable to support the lesser of two evils than to accept the worst with no more than a futile protest vote.

The figures for the New Deal years are slightly above those of the twenties, but these data are, without explanation, somewhat misleading. Many of the third-party votes of 1932, 1934, and 1936, were strictly votes for the Roosevelt program. In some of these races, the Democrats did not even nominate candidates, lest by such action the liberal votes would be divided and the conservatives eke out minority victories. Later, the Democratic strategists, after conferences with liberal third-party leaders, worked out a policy which amounted to practical federalization of the Roosevelt party. The American Labor party (of New York) was fitted into the Democratic plan of campaign, as were the liberals of Minnesota.

The New Deal had no better supporters in its program of social reform than the third-party congressmen from New York, Wisconsin, and Minnesota. Finally, with the partial recovery of the Republicans after 1938, the rather selfish insistence upon their own labels was ameliorated among many members of liberal third parties. If the Democrats really stood for liberalism, and not for the theological morality of the Cleveland era or for human slavery of the Civil War times, there was no objection to being a Democrat. The term "Democrat" lost much of its historical connotation and became, to them, synonymous with reform. In the last three elections, its growing popularity has shown itself in the declining fortunes of third parties.[3]

The same generalizations are supported by the line depicting percentage of contests in which third parties secured as much as 5 per cent of the vote. The highs were 1912, 1914, 1910, 1916, and 1896, and the lows were 1944, 1942, 1930, 1940, and 1928, in that order. Curiously enough, there was no difference in the popularity of third parties between presidential and off-year elections, as in each case the average was 22.9 per cent of the contests in which they polled 5 per cent of the vote.

From these two graph-line trends, it appears that third parties, as real factors in elections, are on the way out and that we will soon realize in purity the principles behind our non-ideological organization of political parties. However, statistical trends are not infallible guides to future developments. What if the North-

[3] The percentage figures for the last two elections were 2.1 and 0.9, which were the lowest for the twenty-five elections.

ern liberals, with labor as a nucleus, refused longer to be tied to the conservatism of Southern politicians and proceeded to form a liberal party in opposition to the Republicans? In that case, another schism, more ominous than that of 1912, would develop, and the Southern Democrats would probably become only a sectional third party which would have such solid backing as to make its absorption into a major party difficult for a very long time.

In the matter of nominating candidates, splinter parties have shown a doggedness and a determination which had little connection with the chances for immediate success. However, the trend is downward, even though the angle of depreciation is not so pronounced as that on popular support. The early highs feature especially the candidates of Populists, Socialists, Socialist Laborites, Prohibitionists, and Progressives. Most of these are now gone, for even the Socialists are now following a plan of "spot" candidacies. They no longer nominate candidates in the strictly rural constituencies, their practice in the first two decades of the period. Only the Communists, either under that name or that of the Workers' party, are optimistic in any marked degree.

The phenomenal upward swing of splinter candidacies in 1930, 1932, 1934, and 1936 sprang from the hope of the extreme left-wingers that the final disintegration of capitalism was near at hand. Mass unemployment, they reasoned, furnished the proper fallow for the seeds of economic radicalism. They fought in the economic as well as in the political field, but after the New Deal tended to discover the limits of its program and some advancement in human security was achieved, the crack-up of capitalism appeared, to the radical elements, to be delayed indefinitely through this opportunism of the Roosevelt coalition. Thereafter, the war became our major task; and though wartimes are, in themselves, conspicuously revolutionary in many social phases, the very urgency of the national effort labels as unpatriotic any tampering with the accepted procedures of economic production. These attitudes account in large part for the spectacular decline in third-party enthusiasm in 1918, 1942, and 1944, our only khaki elections in the fifty-year period.

In only four elections were no third-party candidates elected to the House from single-member constituencies.[4] The longest gap in minor-party success was from 1904 to 1910. It was the period between the Populist and the Progressive movements. In the other twenty-one elections, only 117 minor-party candidates were returned winners. This figure amounts to but 1 per cent of the total contests. The period of the Populists (1896–1902) produced 34; the Progressive era (1910–18), 28; the Artificial Decade (1920–30), 16; and the Roosevelt era (1932–44), 39. The election of 1896 returned 16 and, that of the 1936 chose 12, while those of 1914 and 1934 elected 10 each.

The sectional origins of these successful minor-party congressmen throw considerable light upon the development of our political system. Almost one-half of them (52) came from the Middle West, but that section did not elect its first maverick until 1910. This means that the Populist revolt did not shake the section's solid major-party structure. The break between the Standpat and the Progressive Republicans created the opportunity for third-party candidates. And from 1910 through 1944, only three of the eighteen elections have not witnessed the return of Progressive, Farmer Labor, or Socialist congressmen. However, only Wisconsin and Minnesota, with their indigenous agrarian radicalism, departed from the traditional Republican-Democratic political pattern. All except one of the minor-party congressmen from the Middle West came from these two states.

The West was the particular stronghold of the Populists. From Kansas to the Canadian border and westward to Colorado and Montana, the Populists practically took over the Democratic local organization. From 1896 to 1900 twenty-six western

[4] These were 1904, 1906, 1908, and 1932, but in the last five Farmer Laborites were elected, at large, from Minnesota.

Populists went to the house. The Bull Moose Progressives were also strong in the section. From 1912 to 1920, ten congressmen of that complexion were elected. But since 1920 no third-party candidate has won in any of the fifteen Western states. The East is the third most favorable section for third parties, but no election has selected more than four. And only twenty-one have been chosen in the twenty-five elections. The Bull Moose revolt was the East's most spectacular third-party movement. In the fifty years, the Border has elected no congressman other than a Republican or a Democrat; and the South has contributed only eight, four of whom were Populists. In nineteen of the twenty-five elections, no irregulars were sent up from the twelve Southern states.

In addition to electing more than one hundred congressmen, third parties have exerted a much more important influence upon Congressional elections. Foremost is their polling strength, which would ordinarily go against the party in power. Thus, third parties are generally more harmful to the opposition party than to the party in power. This is shown especially in those contests in which no party is able to secure a majority of the votes. Since 1896, almost 9 per cent (897 contests) have been decided by pluralities rather than by majorities. Of these, the party in power in the lower house at the time of the elections won ten seats for every nine won by the chief opposition party.[5] If control of the presidential office is the criterion, the government won fewer seats than the chief opposition party.[6] Majority winners in the particular elections show about the same 10-9 ratio.[7] This would mean that a higher ratio in winning the close races assists substantially in securing or maintaining the majority status in the House. From a strictly party view, the Republicans won 451 (50.3 per cent), the Democrats 414 (46.1 per cent), and third parties 32 (3.6 per cent).

[5] The percentages are 50.6 and 45.8, with third parties only 3.6.

[6] The percentages here are 46.7 for the government, 49.7 for the chief opposition, and 3.6 for third parties.

[7] The figures are 50.8, 45.6, and 3.6.

These three-way fights determined the control of the House in ten of the twenty-five elections,[8] eight of which came before 1920. This proves again the declining role of minor parties in our political system. Six of the ten elections were won by the Republicans, but that was because the Republicans were winning during the period which followed the Populist-Democratic fusion, and which featured the emergence of modern industrial issues in our politics.

Third parties are playing a prominent part in another phase. In each election, they replace one of the major parties as the principal opposition in several constituencies. The record shows a high of 51 (11.8 per cent) in 1930 and a low of 8 (2.1 per cent) in 1908. The total of 707 constituted 7 per cent of the whole number of contests since 1896. These contests and those in which third parties prevented majority decisions together represent a conspicuous influence. Almost 16 per cent of the total contests since 1896 fall within these categories. Most of the races in which one of the major parties is replaced by a third party occurred in the South.[9]

In a third category, the splinter parties may have exerted

[8] They were 1898, 1902, 1906, 1908, 1910, 1912, 1914, 1916, 1922, and 1930. If the Democrats had won but two of the six plurality contests in 1930, they would have had a majority in the lower house and would not have had to rely upon the fortuitous deaths of Republican congressmen-elect in order to achieve a Democratic majority. In the other very close elections—1916, 1942, 1922, and 1898—the Republicans won more contests than the Democrats. If the Republicans in 1916 had won their 1908 percentage of the sixty-four plurality contests, they would have ended Democratic House control two years earlier than they did.

[9] The South had 318 such contests (44.7 per cent); and most of them were won by the dominant Democratic party by very large majorities. The West was second with 159, followed by the Middle West with 123, the East with 85, and the Border with only 19. The high figure for the West derives especially from the open-primary system of California which permits a single candidate to win the nomination for both major parties. Most of the Middle West's record was amassed in Wisconsin and Minnesota, where the Democrats were elbowed out of the oppositionist role. The low number for the Border proves the very regular character of the party system in those five states.

some influence on the outcome of contests won by a majority vote. This comprises the very large number of races in which one or more third parties offered opposition to both major parties. Since 1896 no less than 4,452 Congressional contests (43.9 per cent) have had minor-party candidates in opposition to both large parties. That they won but thirteen races shows the practical hopelessness of these splinter attempts. Also, it should be remembered that their presence did not prevent a major-party candidate from securing an absolute majority in more than 99 per cent of the contests. Even if their voting support had been added to that of the losing major party, the outcome of the election would not have been altered. Yet in the clash among three or four candidates, voter psychology may well be influenced considerably by the apparent confusion of the campaign. The band-wagon technique may, in such cases, become effective for a major-party candidate. Only then, by raising highly confusing or alarming issues in the campaign, may these minor-party candidates be said to have affected almost one-half of the total number of Congressional contests in the fifty-year period.

The sectional aspects of minor-party influence are important to an understanding of American politics. The sections are fairly consistent in their attitude toward third parties. The East and the Middle West are exactly representative in that their average percentages for the twenty-five elections were identical with that for the entire United States.[10] The West was highest; and the Border and South lowest in that order. Of course, different sections have reacted in dissimilar fashions to particular third-party movements.

To illustrate, the West has, since 1924, been only slightly more generous to third parties than have the Border and the South, but in the years before it led all others in party irregularity. It was twice as potent in Populist votes as any other section.

[10] The percentage for East, Middle West, and United States was 5.3. For the West it was 9.0; for the South and Border, 3.1 and 2.0, respectively.

In fact, for the first three Congressional elections (1896, 1898, and 1900), its percentages of minor-party votes were four times the national averages. Likewise, the Bull Moose schism was more persistent west of the Missouri River than east of it. All sections show large minor-party totals for 1912, but only the West posted a higher figure two years later.[11] Even in 1916, when the other sections had returned to their normal measures of minor-party protest, the West remained unreconciled, as its 10.8 per cent mark reveals.

In the fifteen elections from 1896 to 1924, the West's third-party percentages were ahead of those of all other sections, except in 1910 and 1912. However, from 1926 to 1944 the West was high only in 1932. Thus, the West has been strongest in its support of agricultural revolts, and it was the vanguard in the Populist, Bull Moose, Farmer Labor (1920), and LaFollette Progressive (1924) movements. But the section, having few large industrial centers, contributes very little voter support to the splinter parties which propose panaceas for the more pressing industrial problems.

The East and the Middle West were for the fifty years exactly normal for the entire United States. Each presents an average of 5.3 per cent for the minor-party vote. This was also the national average. Yet the two sections were not identical in their reactions to the various third-party movements. For instance, Populism struck neither of them with much force, but the early Socialist campaigns were much more popular in the East than in the Middle West. Before 1912 the normal third-party percentage in the East was just under 5 per cent; in the Middle West, it was less than 4 per cent. The Bull Moose revolt was of approximately equal strength in the two sections, but through the twenties the Middle West's protest vote is far below that of the East. Beginning in 1930, the Middle West runs

[11] Both the East and the Middle West were slightly above the West's 22.4 per cent in 1912; but in 1914 the West's 23.4 per cent was far ahead of the East's 13.2 per cent and the Middle West's 13.5 per cent.

ahead, sometimes more than double, until the election of 1944. This period of seven elections was featured by the Progressive and the Farmer Labor movements. Neither of them touched the East. Thus, the East's rate of splinter dissent has been more consistent. The Middle West presents generally a much more persistent two-party system. There are only infrequent pockets of preponderant Republican or Democratic strength. Instead, the pattern is that of fairly equal division in the individual constituencies. A similar statement cannot be made about the East, for that section is pitted with many safe constituencies, both Democratic and Republican.

The South stands fourth among the sections in the support of minor parties. Populism shook the foundations of Democratic strength. In fact, the frantic speed with which the franchise qualifications were restricted after the election of 1890 is proof of the respectable white Democrats' alarm over the future prospects. Grandfather's clauses, white primaries, poll taxes, understanding clauses, and other extraordinary qualifications were imposed in order to guarantee that the political power in the South did not fall into the hands of the poorer Negro and white groups. Much has been written about the bars to Negro suffrage in the South, and, without doubt, they exist in very tangible form.[12] But little has been written concerning the practical disfranchisement of white citizens, especially through the poll tax. The point is that the restrictions were imposed as much to remove the threat of white as of Negro radicalism.

The effect of these unusual restrictions was to reduce the electorate to only a fraction of what it would have been without them. Almost one-fifth of the South's 1896 vote was cast for Populist candidates. The revolt continued through 1898 and to some degree until after 1900. The Bull Moose Progressives

[12] Of course, it is not implied that either the grandfather's clause or the white primary is now used to prevent Negroes from voting. Both were declared unconstitutional by the Supreme Court, the first in *Guinn* v. *U. S.* (1915), and the white primary in the Willie Smith case (1944).

picked up scattered support, as the Roosevelt and Taft forces battled throughout the section for control of delegations in the Chicago convention. Louisiana even chose a Progressive congressman in both the 1914 and the 1916 elections. For 1912 the South's third-party total was approximately equal to that of the Republicans, but not all of the former were given to Progressive candidates. Socialists were fairly vocal in many Southern states during this chaotic era. By 1916 the Republican vote was roughly five times that of third parties, and two years later the protests had dwindled to a mere whisper. From 1920 to 1944 the thirteen elections show a practical void in protest, as the average was but 1 per cent. The prevailing party system can scarcely be regarded as in danger if radical splinter groups can command but 1 per cent of the popular vote. Other sections, with freedom of voting, show an average of about 4 per cent. This would, therefore, indicate that restrictions on the suffrage have foiled the plans of the protest groups.

The Border is the most consistent of all sections. The Populist movement touched it scarcely at all, except in Missouri where free silver had a considerable following in the membership of both the major parties. The fundamental political base in the section is that of a stronger Democratic and a weaker Republican strength, the typical election showing some fifty-two Democrats, forty-seven Republicans, and one splinter vote in every hundred voting citizens.

The 1912 Progressives weaned only about one-fourth of the nominal Republicans into the protest ranks, and they apparently won no converts from Democratic ranks. In fact, since 1924, the average third-party strength was only one-third of 1 per cent. That the section has very little industrial activity, except for coal mining, accounts in part for the absence of splinter groups which are found among metropolitan peoples, but this does not explain why the agrarian protest movements developed such sparse strength there. For the most part, the section features a small-holdings' agricultural economy. Moreover, much of it is close to market with its diversified farm products. It is not an outstanding producer of the great surplus farm commodities, such as cotton, corn, or wheat. The very diversification of Border agriculture tends to prevent radicalism among its farmers and to keep them regular in their political allegiances.

Evaluation of the Plurality System

T HE continental extent of the United States tends naturally to nullify the glaring inequities of the single-member constituency system. If the Republicans lose heavily in the South, they win by only slightly less decisiveness in the East and the Middle West. Of the more than 2,600 Congressional contests in the twelve Southern states, the Republicans have won only 4 per cent. On the other hand, in the East, the Middle West, and the West, the Republicans have won two seats for every one lost to the Democrats. Thus, the final count in the House is the fight of a practically unanimous Democratic South against three strongly Republican sections. When the Republicans lose that two-to-one ratio in the three sections, the Democrats win control of Congress.

In contrast to a proportional representation system, our single-member plurality procedure gives no representation to those voters who support losing candidates. Thus it might be theoretically possible for a party with just under one-half of the electorate to receive not a single Congressional post. If the electorate were so uniformly distributed in regard to political convincement, each contest might result in a 51-49 division, and the minority party would have no congressman to represent the millions who voted for its candidates. However, such a postulate is by no means possible in the United States, where the distribution of party strength varies all the way from exclusively Republican to exclusively Democratic constituencies. In every election, there are many Democrats (chiefly in the South) and a few Republicans who are returned without opposition.

For the 10,148 single-member races, the average quota of the Democrats was the smallest, with that for the Republicans approximately 9 per cent larger, and with that for all third parties more than 300 per cent larger.[1] The South again substantially influences these averages, for that section's Democratic quota was but one-third the national Democratic quota, while the Southern Republican one was twice its national average. For the 7,500 congressmen elected from the other four sections, the Republican quota was 54,279, while that of the Democrats was 84,132 (or 55 per cent larger). Thus, the non-South Democratic average quota was almost 62 per cent larger than the national quota for that party.

An examination of the sectional records will go far to explain the basis of American politics. The fundamental trends are more easily discovered through focusing attention upon particular parts of the whole picture. Political trends may move in opposite directions in different sections. They may move at different speeds and thus alter the political balance in the United States.

EAST

The East has been a predominately Republican section. Of its 2,863 contests, that party has accounted for 66.2 per cent, the Democrats for 33 per cent, and other parties for but four-fifths of 1 per cent. Of the twenty-five, the Democrats have won a majority of seats in but three elections.[2] In 1940 the two major parties each took 59 contests. But in the remaining 21 elections, the Republicans carried the section. In 1896 the Democrats won only nine of the ninety-seven seats. Since 1920 the urban centers, and especially New York City, have sent many more Democrats to the House than prior to that time. In fact, of the 1,419 races from 1896 to 1920, inclusive, the Republicans won about 72 per cent, while the Democrats secured less than

[1] The exact figures are Democratic, 51,983; Republican, 56,592; others, 209,313; and average, 56,059.
[2] These three were 1912, 1934, and 1936.

27 per cent.[3] Since 1920, of every ten seats, the Republicans have won six and the Democrats four. More than one-half of the East's Democratic congressmen since 1920 have come from the state of New York, though the Roosevelt revolution of 1932 loosed the grip of the Republicans upon other states. And by 1934 even rock-ribbed Republican Pennsylvania was more than two-to-one Democratic in its congressional representation.[4] Not until 1938 did the section return to its traditional Republican complexion, and even then the Democrats received 40 per cent of the seats. Only Maine and Vermont were unshaken by this Democratic upsurge. In the urban districts of Massachusetts, Rhode Island, Connecticut, and New Jersey, the dominance of the Republicans was challenged with the same spirit as in the Pennsylvania cities.

The tenacity of the East's Republican strength is proved in the twenty-one elections in which the Republicans won a majority of the House seats.[5] However, the sharp improvement in Democratic fortunes in the last seven elections records the changing character of the section's politics. Prior to 1932 the East's political preference had been that of the entire United States in fifteen of the eighteen elections, and in those other three (1910, 1914, and 1916) the Democrats had won approximately one-third of the section's seats, an increase of 50 per cent over the average Democratic delegation in the seven elections before 1910. However, the twenties, wherein the Republicans won a majority in each of the five elections, found the Democrats improving their lot slightly. They were usually around

[3] Of the 302 Democratic seats won, 196 came from New York state, especially from the urban districts in New York City, where the Tammany Democratic organization has, ever since the Civil War, constituted the largest and most important Democratic pocket in any of the three Republican sections.

[4] The 1934 Pennsylvania elections chose eleven Republicans and twenty-three Democrats; those of 1936 selected seven Republicans and twenty-seven Democrats. These figures contrast strangely with those for 1926, when the Democrats took but one of Pennsylvania's thirty-six districts.

[5] The section's record in seats won, 1896–1944, is shown on page 83.

the one-third mark, a distinct improvement over the period immediately following the great Populist revolt. The people of the section had been fearful of agricultural radicalism. The twenties found them reacting somewhat more favorably to the still small voice of industrial radicalism.

The greatest losses in Congressional representation were by the Republicans in 1898, 1910, 1912, 1932, and 1934, and by the Democrats in 1900, 1914, 1920, 1938, and 1942.[6] Losses for the majority party mean automatic gains for the opposition. Of course, percentage figures for these gains and losses are subject to interpretation, for losses from a safe majority will mean a reasonably small percentage figure, while gains from an insignificant number may roll up a spectacular figure. In 1898 the Democratic gain was almost 250 per cent, but even then the Republicans had more than two-thirds of the Eastern congressmen. The Democrats won but nine seats in 1896. In the 1898 election, the Republicans lost twenty-one of their delegation to the Democrats, but the Republican loss was less than 25 per cent. This demonstrates the very obvious danger in utilizing what my friend Clarence Nixon calls "lumber-camp" statistics. His story is that, in a camp of one hundred male laborers and two women cooks, an ordinary marriage between one of the workers and a cook was reported by an enterprising young secretary with a flair for statistics as a marriage between 1 per cent of the men and 50 per cent of the women. Election statistics are subject to similar misinterpretation.

Being distinctly a minority party in the East, the Democrats

[6] The losses and gains in representation for these spot years were:

Year	Rep. Loss	Dem. Gain	Year	Dem. Loss	Rep. Gain
1898	24.2%	247.8%	1900	29.1%	16.6%
1910	24.1	74.6	1914	51.6	94.3
1912	40.1	56.5	1920	52.2	17.2
1922	25.6	199.2	1938	33.4	48.9
1932	22.8	54.9	1942	23.6	23.4
1934	24.5	29.5			

Note 5, page 81.

EAST

Year	1896	98	1900	02	04	06	08	10	12	14	16	18	20	22	24	26	28	30	32	34	36	38	40	42	44	96–44
Republican	87	66	75	75	90	80	83	63	42	81	87	88	104	80	93	91	92	87	65	49	47	70	59	71	69	1894
Democrat	9	31	22	29	17	27	24	42	73	35	30	29	14	43	28	32	31	36	54	70	72	48	59	44	49	948
Others	1			3				2	4	2	2	1	1		1							1	1	1	1	21
All	97	97	97	107	107	107	107	107	119	118	119	118	119	123	122	123	123	123	119	119	119	119	119	116	119	2863

Note 10, page 86.

BORDER

Year	1896	98	1900	02	04	06	08	10	12	14	16	18	20	22	24	26	28	30	32	34	36	38	40	42	44	96–44
Republican	17	13	13	11	20	18	17	8	7	8	10	17	13	27	18	15	26	11		2	2	4	4	15	9	307
Democrat	20	24	24	28	19	21	22	31	32	31	30	23	27	13	22	25	14	29	13	33	33	31	31	20	26	621
All	37	37	37	39	39	39	39	39	39	39	40	40	40	40	40	40	40	40	13	35	35	35	35	35	35	928

83

have been penalized through the operation of the single-member constituency system. Their average quota for each congressman elected is 72 per cent larger than that for the Republicans.[7] If seats had been awarded on the basis of votes cast, the Democrats would have increased their number of congressmen by almost 35 per cent.[8] Of course, third parties suffered most, as they earned 140 and received only 21. Naturally, the Republicans as the major party of the section received more than their proportional share. The plurality system increased their number of victories by approximately one-third.[9] Only in the three elections in which the Democrats won a majority of the seats was their quota smaller than that of the Republicans, and even then there was less disparity in the quotas than was generally the case in normal Republican victories. In 1940, the closest election in the section, when each major party won fifty-nine seats, the Democratic quota was less than 1 per cent larger than that of the Republicans. However, the usual pattern for the section's politics is that the Republicans have smaller pluralities in the rural areas than the Democrats in the cities. This militated against the Democrats, as there were more rural constituencies. In recent decades the increase of urbanization in the section has improved Democratic fortunes, though there appears some evidences in recent elections that the Democrats may be caught in the same political squeeze which practically destroyed the Liberal party in Great Britain. They may not be able to satisfy the demands of labor in their national program. The American Labor party, as yet concentrated in New York City, may well become the nucleus of a new political movement throughout the section.

For the most part, the section's politics have been reasonably

[7] The Republican quota was 50,276 votes, while the Democratic one was 86,408.

[8] They would have had 1,278 rather than the 948 which they actually won in the single-member races.

[9] They received 1,894 as against 1,445, which would have been their proportional share.

steady. The normal year saw some eighty to ninety Republican congressmen and from twenty-five to forty-five Democratic victories, even though in popular votes the Republican total was but 13 per cent larger than that of the Democrats. As we have already noted in the clash of parties in the single-member contests, the Republicans emerged conspicuous victors in the East. Of almost fifteen hundred races in which there were fewer than twenty percentage points between winner and nearest loser, or races inside the sixty-four distribution limits, the Republicans won 62 per cent and the Democrats less than 36 per cent. One-half of the Republican victories were in this category.

Where there is fairly even distribution of political strength throughout a section, the plurality system works to the tremendous advantage of the majority party. The election of 1908 was fairly typical of the campaigns before the emergence of the New Deal era. The Republicans cast approximately 55 per cent of the popular votes, but they received almost 78 per cent of the seats. The Democrats got but 22 per cent of the seats with more than 40 per cent of the vote. Here are the dynamics that make for safe majorities in the House of Representatives.

A study of the effect of gain or loss of popular votes upon the number of seats won will reveal no hard and fast arithmetic formula. In the ten elections, in which the majority party polled a smaller percentage of popular votes than two years before, the average loss in representation was 2.5 per cent for every percentage-point loss in popular votes. The average gain (in thirteen elections) was 3.6 per cent in representation for every percentage point gained in popular vote. Of course, there were abnormal years, such as 1912, when a 12 per cent gain in Democratic popular vote netted a 95 per cent gain in Congressional seats. The competition of third parties produced this unusual phenomenon. However, if one takes only the fluctuations in the 45 per cent to 55 per cent group, the net gain or loss is 3.3 per cent in representation for every percentage-point change in popular vote.

Also, gains in popular vote for the chief opposition party, barring strong third-party activity, will not be so much if the gain does not bring the total up to around the 40 per cent mark. For instance, in 1926 the Democrats, a poor second in the election, increased their vote by 6 per cent over 1924, but they improved their representation only from twenty-eight to thirty-two seats. On the other hand, a like gain by the Democrats in 1940 increased their representation from forty-eight to fifty-nine. And a Republican loss of just over 4 per cent in 1934 reduced the party delegation from sixty-five to forty-nine. A Republican loss of less than 8 per cent in 1932 took twenty-two of the party's eighty-seven congressmen out of the legislative halls. The standing of the party experiencing the gain or loss is the most important factor in the operation of the plurality system, as it gives a party no more representation to win a constituency with a plurality of 40 per cent rather than with 1 per cent.

If the parties had been awarded seats in proportion to popular votes, the Republicans' total would have been reduced to 1,445 from 1,894, the Democrats' 948 would have been boosted to 1,278, and the third parties' 21 would have been upped to 140.

BORDER

The five Border states occupy the median position between the practically unanimous Democratic South and the Republican East and Middle West.[10] In ordinary times the section is Democratic, but the Republican minority is articulate and tenacious. On only two occasions (1912 and 1936) have the Republicans received less than 40 per cent of the popular vote. In fifteen of the twenty-five elections, the Republican minority polled more than 45 per cent of the vote. And on three occasions (1904, 1920, and 1928), the traditional minority party won more congressional posts than the Democrats.[11] It should be noted that these three Republican victories came in presidential elec-

[10] The record of the sections in party success is shown on page 83.

tion years. In the other five elections, four of them in the New Deal era, the Republican percentages were between 40 and 45.

Though the Republicans polled about 46 per cent of the total popular vote for the half-century, they won only 32 per cent of the Congressional seats. Thus, the Democrats took 68 per cent of the races with less than 52 per cent of the votes. The plurality system renders it possible for pronounced shifts in the party complexions of the Congressional delegations with only slight alterations in the popular vote. This is especially true where there are few pockets of overwhelming single-party strength. The East, with its Democratic pocket in New York City, seldom saw extremely violent shifts in party fortunes. The Border has few safe seats for either of the major parties. Kentucky is the one exception to this general rule. It has a safe Republican district, and some five or six safe Democratic seats. But the other four states, though leaning generally to the Democrats, have strong and fairly evenly distributed Republican strength.

Only a slight shift among the voters results in pronounced changes in the election results. In 1904, a 3 per cent shift produced a 25 per cent switch in Congressional representation. In 1910 a gain of less than 1 per cent took nine of the section's thirty-nine seats from the Republicans. In 1928, a 5 per cent Democratic loss took eleven seats, and two years later a 6 per cent Republican loss returned not only the eleven to the Democrats, but four others were tossed in for good measure. And in 1932 another 6 per cent Republican loss wiped out completely the minority-party representation.[12]

11 In 1904 the Republicans won only twenty of the thirty-nine seats, and their popular vote (49.8 per cent) was only three-tenths of 1 per cent above that of the Democrats. In the other two elections, the Republican victories were clear cut, as the 52 per cent (1920) and 53.5 per cent (1928) were far ahead of the 46.3 per cent and 46.4 per cent of the Democrats.

12 It should be noted that both Kentucky and Missouri elected their congressmen in at-large elections in 1932. When these states returned to single-member constituencies in 1934, the Republicans won two seats with a slightly smaller percentage of popular votes.

Of the last seven elections, only that of 1942 saw the Republicans secure more than their average number of seats. In both popular vote and representation, the party's fortunes were at their lowest ebb in the entire fifty-year period. Even though they continued to poll from one and one-quarter to one and three-quarter million votes, the Democrats were definitely gaining ground at their expense. Of course, the plurality system gave a distinct advantage to the Democrats. The average Democratic Congressional vote-quota of 47,380 contrasts conspicuously with the Republican average of 84,537. In 1936 the Republicans received one congressman for every 842,356 votes and the Democrats one for every 76,221 votes. Even in 1944 the Democratic quota was but 40 per cent of that of the Republicans.[13]

The section has contributed substantially to Democratic success. In the eleven elections in which that party won Congressional majorities, more than 80 per cent of the Border's congressmen were members of the Democratic caucus. The conspicuous exception was in 1942, when almost 43 per cent of the Border seats went to the Republicans. In the fourteen years of Republican national victory, just under 44 per cent of the seats went to that party. Though small in population, the Border may well determine the national winner.

SOUTH

The South is a section apart from the national political scene. It fits none of the dominant national political characteristics. It is a one-party section. Of its 2,638 constituency contests of the last fifty years, no less than 2,518 (95.4 per cent) were won by the Democrats.[14] The Republican total of 112 means that their Southern average was only four and one-half House seats in each of the twenty-five congresses. Curiously enough, with this insignificant average, the Republicans have never been without

[13] The figures were 77,772 for the Democrats and 192,796 for the Republicans.

[14] The party success record is shown on page 91.

Southern representation, though in each 1906, 1932, 1934, 1936, and 1938 there were only two Southern Republicans elected to the House.[15] The years of Republican highs were 1920, with eleven seats, and 1928, with ten. However, the only safe Republican constituency is the "old first" of Tennessee, where Democrats rarely take the trouble to nominate a candidate. Oklahoma usually elects a Republican from the district which lies next to the Kansas border, and North Carolina has sent an occasional Republican to Washington from one of its mountain constituencies.

The wastage in minority-party votes is not nearly so important in the South as in the East, for neither the Republicans nor third parties have any appreciable strength from Virginia to Texas. The Democrats have polled more than 70 per cent of the vote during the period. With this, they have taken 95 per cent of the Congressional seats. The statistics sound impressive, but the control of the dominant party is so certain that non-Democratic candidates cause no flurries in election campaigns. One result of this almost absolute hegemony is that the Democratic primary campaigns present the political pyrotechnics to Southern voters. And the Democratic party, for that reason, can have no definite program that would distinguish it from an opposition. It is both the majority party and the opposition rolled into one catholic organization. Liberal Democrats vie with conservative Democrats for the party nominations and certain election in November. Under such conditions, each Congressional district is an ideological unit within itself. The term "Democrat" assumes a generic cast, and carries a connotation in the South not unlike the term "American" in the other sections. Practically all electors are registered as Democrats. As such they participate in the Democratic primaries. To register as a Republican would constitute practical disfranchisement to a citizen, especially in

[15] The years in which only three were elected were 1902, 1922, 1940, and 1942; those with only four were 1898, 1900, 1904, 1918, 1924, 1926, 1930 and 1944.

the field of local elections. Where party nomination is synony-mous to election, the citizen, if he is to register an intelligent choice, must do so at the level at which the actual selection is consummated. This major-party registration of those who, un-der different circumstances would be in the official opposition parties, in reality destroys the entire justification for the exist-ence of the party system.

The party system is supposed to furnish the mechanics for organizing opinion and presenting the means for the orderly decision of the citizenry in representative government. With its present legal and customary restrictions upon the franchise, the South has destroyed—if indeed it ever existed there at the mass level—the party system. No opposition party has any re-spectable standing. An independent will draw as many votes in the usual Southern general election as a Republican. And most of the meagre third-party votes (amounting to only slightly over 2 per cent for the half-century) were cast for independent candidates. Some of these were by the "die-hards" whose candi-dates were defeated at the nomination stage.

In about a dozen constituencies of the section, formal Re-publican local organization is continuously alive and vital. Most of these lie in the Appalachian districts of the old South, where modern Jeffersonians persist in their ideas of liberty. In addition, three Oklahoma districts have solid Republican organization. In Oklahoma, however, the percentage of registered Republi-cans is very low, though a Republican candidate for United States senator or governor will, under normal political circum-stances, poll approximately 40 per cent of the state vote. Most of the support comes from registered Democrats whose personal candidates were defeated in the primary. In the New Deal era, the difference between a conservative Democrat and a conserva-tive Republican was more apparent than real. Upon the election of an anti-Roosevelt Democrat as governor, the Republican na-tional committeeman for Oklahoma remarked that his party had, ever since statehood (1906), been trying to elect a governor and

Note 14, page 88.

SOUTH

Year	1896	98	1900	02	04	06	08	10	12	14	16	18	20	22	24	26	28	30	32	34	36	38	40	42	44	96–44
Republican	8	4	4	3	4	2	9	5	5	5	5	4	11	3	4	4	10	4	2	2	2	2	3	3	4	112
Democrat	79	85	86	95	94	96	94	98	100	103	104	108	101	109	108	108	101	107	95	107	108	108	106	109	109	2518
Other	3	1									1						1			1			1		1	8
All	90	90	90	98	98	98	103	103	105	108	109	112	112	112	112	112	112	111	97	109	110	110	112	112	113	2638

Note 17, page 92.

MIDDLE WEST

Year	1896	98	1900	02	04	06	08	10	12	14	16	18	20	22	24	26	28	30	32	34	36	38	40	42	44	96–44
Republican	79	79	79	81	97	83	73	59	44	69	79	90	101	83	86	88	92	73	28	32	25	63	64	79	73	1802
Democrat	17	17	17	21	5	19	29	42	58	34	25	13	3	19	14	14	12	31	67	62	67	38	35	20	28	700
Others								1		2	1	2	3	5	3	1	1	10	12	3	5	3	1			57
All	96	96	96	102	102	102	102	102	102	105	105	105	104	105	105	105	105	105	95	104	104	104	104	102	102	2559

Note 20, page 95.

WEST

Year	1896	98	1900	02	04	06	08	10	12	14	16	18	20	22	24	26	28	30	32	34	36	38	40	42	44	96–44
Republican	13	18	20	24	29	29	28	28	26	25	27	43	47	42	42	41	45	41	14	14	12	24	27	35	35	729
Democrat	5	4	4	6	1	2	6	6	15	19	21	9	5	11	11	8	12	13	43	43	45	33	30	22	22	396
Others	12	8	6		2				5		1	1	1													35
All	30	30	30	30	31	34	34	43	49	53	53	53	53	53	53	53	53	53	57	57	57	57	57	57	57	1160

that he was pleased to announce that that aspiration was finally realized. Conditions such as these foster very unsettled and irresponsible politics.

The result of these circumstances is that the section's voting-participation rate is far below that of the remainder of the United States.[16] Citizens who would in a reasonably free political order join a minority party and strive for the implementation of its program either cannot qualify for the franchise or accept the hopelessness of the situation and remain away from the polling places. In nine-tenths of the constituencies there is nothing that resembles a political contest on general election day. Since 1920 there have been no less than 579 unopposed candidates, an average of 43 ½ per cent of the seats for the thirteen elections. Moreover, in a preponderant majority of the remaining contests, the opposition strength was so negligible as to offer no real opposition to the Democratic candidates.

The South's average Republican quota was six times that of the Democrats. If the Republicans had received representation on an absolutely equitable basis with the Democrats, they would have had 713 rather than the 112 seats which they actually secured. By the same criterion the Democrats would have elected 1,865 rather than 2,518.

MIDDLE WEST

The hinterland from Pittsburgh to Omaha, and from the Ohio River to the Great Lakes has been the "most Republican" section of the United States. Its 70.4 per cent mark in Republican victories[17] does not approach the 95.4 per cent Democratic mark in the South, but it exceeds both the East and the West with their respective Republican percentages of 66.2 and 62.8. The Middle West has been "too Republican," as the Border has been

[16] This does not apply to Oklahoma, which presents a very respectable participation rate.

[17] The section has returned 1,802 Republicans, 700 Democrats, and 57 third-party congressmen. The detailed record is shown on page 91.

"too Democratic," to serve as a fair index of national politics. Since 1930 the West has been nearer the national trend, but before that the Middle West was closest to the norm.

In the twenty-five congresses, the section has given a majority of its seats to the party in power on seventeen occasions. In the fourteen Republican congresses, the average Democratic take from the Middle West was but 15 per cent, or almost six Republican congressmen for every Democratic one. In the eleven Democratic congresses, the majority party took an average of 42 per cent of the section's posts. If the Democrats can win from thirty-five to forty Midwestern seats, they have an excellent chance to win majority control of the House. Of the fourteen Republican triumphs, only in 1930—a very close race in the entire country—did the Republican majority party fall below the 70 per cent mark in the Middle West. That seems to be the danger mark for the Republicans.

This does not imply that the Democrats, as the section's traditional minor party, did not make a good showing at the polls: in seventeen of the elections they polled more than 40 per cent of the popular vote. But the distribution of Republican strength was so general as to reduce the efficacy of the Democratic vote. In ten of the elections the Republicans cast between 50 and 55 per cent of the vote, but they averaged three-fourths of the Congressional seats. This reveals how effectively the plurality system deprives the minor party of its representation out of all equitable proportion.

Since 1928 the Republicans have received fewer seats, even with usual popular-vote percentages. The rapid growth of large urban centers, especially in the Great Lakes region, has produced a number of fairly safe Democratic constituencies. So long as organized labor remains an integral part of the Democratic party, this altered condition will remain the political pattern. The powerful Democratic machine in Cook County, Illinois, constitutes a fortress of the Democratic strength in Illinois; it has been enough, with some assistance from down state, to carry

Illinois in presidential contests and to send sizable Democratic delegations to the House.

In no other section has third-party strength cut so deeply into that of the regular minor party. In the three easternmost of the seven states of the section, the spread of Democratic strength is evener than in the other four states; and it was sufficient to come to power in periods of embarrassment for the majority party. These states have developed no permanent third parties, though, of course, the Progressive schism of 1912 captured approximately one-fourth of the Republican voters, but it also reduced by 10 per cent the vote of the Democrats. In both Wisconsin and Minnesota, where the minor party was never strong, the natural development was a split in the Republican ranks. There are now evidences that the Rooseveltian era has increased the Democrats in those states so much as to heal the schism in the Republican party.[18] This represents one of the laws of American politics, where the franchise is free and few impediments are offered to the organization of new parties. There is little doubt that, under similar conditions, the Democratic party in the South would have split into two almost equally strong parties.

The section's average Republican quota was slightly less than one-half that of the Democrats, and only one-third of the third-party figure.[19] If the average quota for all parties had been sustained throughout, the total Republican seats would have been reduced from 1,802 to 1,338, the Democratic total would have risen from 700 to 1,089, and the third-party victories from 57 to 132.

If the battle in the Middle West returns to its traditional Republican-Democratic character, we may expect a somewhat closer struggle. The migration of thousands of citizens from

[18] As this is written, the LaFollette Progressives have formally returned to the Republican party in Wisconsin.

[19] The average quotas for the three were: Republican, 52,121; Democratic, 107,336; and third parties, 154,183.

Kentucky, West Virginia, and Tennessee into the heavy-industry centers of the section will contribute to an increase for the Democrats. The Negro vote is also important in Ohio, Indiana, Michigan, and Illinois; it supported Franklin D. Roosevelt generally. However, if the adamancy of the Southern die-hards continues to block the Negro drive for political and economic equality throughout the United States, it is practically inevitable that this numerous group, now fairly cohesive politically, will return to Republican ranks. A development such as this would again put the Republicans safely ahead of the Democrats in the section.

WEST

The political picture in the West is more like that of the Middle West than of any other section. In twenty of the twenty-five elections, it gave the Republicans more Congressional seats than it gave any other party.[20] Even during the Wilson era it remained a Republican section, though the usual high percentages were steeply reduced. The first break came in 1932. The Democrats carried the section in the first five F.D.R. Congressional elections. The Republicans came back to win in 1942 and 1944, but their percentages were far below those of the twenties. In fact, the West now stands, so far as the distribution of party strength is concerned, about where it was in 1912 and 1914, years of Republican sickness.

The Western states were the fortress of Populist strength. For the first three congresses of the period, the section returned more Populist and Fusion candidates than Democrats to House seats. Thereafter the protestants split, some going to each of the major parties, although the Republican nucleus was larger. The accretion placed the Republicans out of serious danger from Democratic challenge. In 1904 only one Democratic congressman was elected from the thirteen states.[21] Two years later two

[20] The section has elected 729 Republicans, 396 Democrats, and 35 third-party congressmen. The detailed record is shown on page 91.
[21] New Mexico and Arizona had not yet come into the Union.

Democrats were returned. Moreover, even after the four Democratic congresses of the teens (1910–16), the minority party was still weak and uncertain. In 1920 only five Democrats, in contrast to forty-seven Republicans, were elected. During the Hoover landslide (1928) the numbers were eight and forty-five. These figures emphasize the distinctly inferior position occupied by the Democrats during three-fourths of the period.

The New Deal years practically switched the positions of the major parties. Before 1932 New Mexico, Arizona, and Nevada were regarded as the Democratic states, with almost equal chances between the parties in Utah and Montana. But in late years the Pacific coast states have altered their traditional habit of Republican allegiance, and are now returning an almost equal number of Democratic congressmen. Both Washington and California are developing urban centers of considerable size, and the usual improvement in Democratic strength has resulted. As a counterdevelopment, the old Populist stretches of the wheat country are moving back to being safe Republican constituencies, even though they were very favorable to the Roosevelt program in the earlier days of the New Deal.

As in the Middle West, the plurality system has operated to the advantage of the Republicans. Their average quota was but two-thirds that of the Democrats. If each party had received seats on the basis of votes cast, the Republican total of 729 would have been cut to 607, the Democratic total of 396 would have been raised to 494, and third parties would have received 59 rather than the 35 which they actually secured.

THE COMPOSITE PICTURE

When the five sections are drawn together into the national political unit, an unusually interesting picture is presented. The inequities of the individual sections are, for the most part, erased in the statistical canceling which occurs among the sectional units. The pertinent figures for average quotas per Congressional seat in the twenty-five elections are shown on page 97.

RELATION BETWEEN SEATS *EARNED AND WON* BY PARTIES AND SECTIONS

	Republican		Democrats		Third Parties		All Parties	Seats Earned			Relation of Won to Earned Seats %		
	Quota	Seats Won	Quota	Seats Won	Quota	Seats Won	Average Quota	Rep.	Dem.	Others	Rep.	Dem.	Others
East	50,276	1894	86,408	948	389,425	21	64,722	1445	1278	140	+31.0	−25.8	−85.0
Border	84,537	307	47,380	621	840,946	0	56,050	425	479	24	−27.8	+29.6	−100.0
South	113,668	112	18,126	2518	247,812	8	22,879	713	1865	60	−84.3	+35.0	−86.7
Middle West	52,121	1802	107,336	700	154,183	57	69,498	1338	1089	132	+34.7	−36.0	−58.3
West	63,526	729	94,471	396	158,775	35	76,869	607	494	59	+20.1	−19.8	−40.9
U. S.	56,592	4844	51,983	5183	209,313	121	56,059	4528	5205	415	+ 6.98	− 0.4	−70.8

The table shows that the Republicans, by favorable distribution of party strength, received more seats than they were entitled to on the basis of popular votes in three sections—the East, the Middle West, and the West. The Democrats were overrepresented in the South and the Border. Of course, no system of representation, not even proportional representation, gives seats to parties on the absolutely equitable basis of voting strength. Even the German list system, with its transfer of excess quota fractions to higher lists, failed to give absolutely equitable distribution.

Curiously enough, the American fifty-year record of single-member constituency contests approaches the ideal to an amazing degree. The Democrats lacked less than one-half of 1 per cent of securing their equitable number of seats. They lacked only 21 of the 10,148 seats of getting their absolute proportion. The Republicans received 316 more than they were entitled to under the proportional standard. These came almost wholly from third parties, which lacked 294 of getting their proper share. It should be remembered, however, that these third-party vote totals were made up largely of splinter votes, of totals which were in most cases under the 5 per cent mark in individual contests. There were also many separate splinter groups which made their contributions to the cumulative total. To grant them representation on such showings would be ludicrous in any political system.

SOME CHARACTERISTICS OF THE PLURALITY SYSTEM

The fundamental law of the plurality system is that those receiving a majority of votes in a particular contest are the winners and the minority retains only the right to become the majority in the next election. We have seen how nearly the two major parties came to receiving their proper number of Congressional seats, from a strictly proportional standard. But those figures were no more than the summation of sectional statistics, in which the inequities in the particular sections neutralized one another and produced a generalization derived from contradictory details.

The same favorable generalization is shown by taking the national Congressional vote percentages for the two parties for the twenty-five elections. Dividing them into majority and minority groups and correlating each with the percentage of representation received, any defender of the plurality system would find the results unbelievably satisfactory. The twenty-five majority-vote percentages (both Republican and Democratic) received an average of 1.14 per cent of representation for every per cent of popular vote. The twenty-five minority-vote percentages received representation on the basis of 0.93 per cent for every percentage of popular vote. Yet here the South, when in the minority in the years of Republican victory, boosted the minority representation figures beyond their reasonable level. These statistics are like those derived from the application of the overall proportional standard.

A much better view of the plurality system is to be had from a consideration of the sectional aspects. Here sectional majorities and minorities are correlated. Thus the Democratic votes of the South would always be in the majority column. No dissenting sections could jumble the results by offsetting one inequitable allocation of representation against another, by posing the South against the Middle West and thus getting an erroneous but apparently fair result.

The election returns show that every per cent of popular vote polled by majority parties in individual sections captured no less than 1.33 per cent of the Congressional representation;[22] that is, the majority-party vote percentage took its proportional share and one-third of another seat, which by the proportional standard belonged to minor parties. This spread accounts for safe majorities in the House for parties which polled only a slight

[22] The sectional figures for majority parties' correlation between popular votes and representations (based upon popular-vote percentages of representation percentages) are shown at the foot of page 100:

majority of the popular votes. Of course, the unequal distribution of party strength in a section accounts altogether for the fact that the majority party did not take all of the representation. The most effective category was that from 55 to 66 per cent, as it won 1.5 per cent of the representation with every percentage of its vote. This does not mean that higher categories of majority strength did not roll up large House majorities. They did, but the percentage of representation won does not increase so fast as the increase in popular votes.

The minority figures naturally fit into this statistical pattern.[23] The average representation is just under 0.5 per cent for every percentage of popular vote. The discrimination here is very obvious. The South dominates the category of below 40 per cent, though sixteen of the West's elections were also in this group. Both the East and the Middle West were strong in the 40–45 per cent class, and the Border had eighteen elections in the 45 to 49 per cent category. This last class is so close to the majority line that, naturally, it would reap much higher rewards than those below it. A party which runs so close to victory has an almost equal chance of dividing the seats and could, with favorable distribution of strength, win a majority of the seats. As a matter of fact, this happened four times in the

	0–50	50–55	55–60	60–99	0–99
East	1.20	1.26	1.34	1.45	1.29
Border	1.05	1.33	1.61		1.35
South			1.49	1.27	1.28
Middle West	1.31	1.42	1.43	1.38	1.40
West	1.21	1.39	1.50	1.29	1.35
United States	1.20	1.35	1.46	1.29	1.33

[23] The sectional minority-parties' vote percentages of representation percentages were as follows:

	0–40	40–45	45–49.3	0–49.3
East	0.60	0.72	0.94	0.74
Border	0.24	0.23	0.77	0.64
South	0.19			0.19
Middle West	0.42	0.61	0.62	0.55
West	0.60	0.51	0.93	0.65
United States	0.42	0.58	0.81	0.48

fifty years. An illustration is that the Republicans in the East in 1932 won a majority of seats with only 47.7 per cent of the popular vote.[24]

The discrimination increases in the categories of small minority votes. For instance, where the minority vote does not exceed 20 per cent of the total, the representation secured is only one-fourth of the vote ratio. Thus, if a party got only 24 per cent of the vote, it would, by the law of the averages, receive only 6 per cent of the representation.[25] Oddly enough, the ratio of representation does not increase from the 0.25 per cent until the minority passes the 30 per cent grade in popular vote. Then it doubles. The obvious explanation here is that a few minority pockets are within the category of safe seats, and that the minority does not really begin to challenge majority control in the other constituencies until it can command in the neighborhood of one-third of the popular votes; for a general average of one-third would, under usual degrees of individual constituency variation, mean that some constituencies would have much higher minority-party strength.

SECTIONAL CONTRIBUTIONS TO PARTY VICTORY

To secure a majority in the House, the Republicans must win a majority of seats in at least three sections—East, Middle West, and West. Eleven of their fourteen victories have featured that combination.[26] In the other three elections, the Border joined with the three Republican sections to constitute the majority.[27] If the Border goes Republican, the party majority is overwhelming. The combined score for these three elections was 64.3 per cent for the Republicans and 35.5 per cent for the

[24] It recurred also once each in the Border, the Middle West, and the West.

[25] There are, of course, examples of greater injustice; for instance, the South has on three occasions been given less than 2 per cent of the representation for more than 17 per cent of the popular vote.

[26] These were 1896, 1898, 1900, 1902, 1906, 1908, 1918, 1922, 1924, 1926, and 1930.

[27] 1904, 1920, and 1928.

Democrats. These were the great landslide victories of the Republicans, all in presidential years, in which they polled an average percentage of the Congressional vote of 55.9. If the Border goes with the Republicans, it is practically certain to produce a landslide Republican victory.

Republican pluralities in the three Republican sections are not, unless sizable, sufficient to give the party a House majority. As a matter of fact, in five of the eleven Democratic triumphs the Republicans carried these three sections, but they lost too many seats to the minority candidates.[28] The average Republican votes in each of the three sections were from seven to eight percentage points above the Democrats, and the ratio of seats won was two to one in their favor. But that one-third of the seats in the three sections was enough to give national victory to the Democrats.

In the eleven elections in which the Republicans won by carrying only the three Republican sections, their average percentage was 55.5 as against only 37.9 for the Democrats. Therefore, the statistical rule is that the Republicans must carry the East, the Middle West, and the West by more than 55 per cent of the popular vote if they are to eke out a majority in the House. Even in the election of 1930, which they won by a slight majority, the Republicans polled from 54.3 per cent in the West to 56.6 per cent in the Middle West. Of course, third parties had practically no influence on this election. The Republican percentage must be higher if third parties are not prominent in the election, for third parties usually reduce substantially the votes of the traditional minor party, such as the Democratic party, in these three sections.

With 55 per cent of the popular vote in the East, the Republicans should win from 85 to 90 seats; with the same percentage in the Middle West, they should win from 77 to 82 seats; and the West should give around 40 seats for that percentage. Under such conditions 15 seats are likely to be picked up in the Border

[28] 1910, 1914, 1916, 1942, and 1944.

and 4 or 5 in the South. Even with minimum calculations, the party would have 221 posts. This would be a close victory. Without third-party influence, it would not likely occur unless the party polled a full 55 per cent of the popular vote in the three sections.

The Democrats can start every campaign with the knowledge that more than 100 Democratic congressmen will come, almost with opposition, from the South. Even in the Hoover landslide of 1928, the South sent 101 Democratic House members to Washington. In the seven New Deal elections, their number has fluctuated only between 106 (1940) and 109 (1942 and 1944). To this number, the Border will add 25 under normal conditions. In addition, if political circumstances are favorable, from 4 to 7 more will be added to the Democratic roster. Thus, the Democrats have a nucleus of around 130 seats before they invade the three Republican sections.

The Democrats would need to pick up but 88 of the 278 seats in the three remaining sections. Under present conditions, from 35 to 40 are reasonably sure from the East. This would leave a maximum of only 53 from the Middle West and the West. Chicago, Detroit, and Cleveland should elect a minimum of from 20 to 25. If the latter figure is accurate, the Democrats would need but 28 for a majority. That number is quite possible in the West, with the traditional Democratic strength in New Mexico, Arizona, and Nevada, and the newly rising urban communities in California and Washington. Even if the West should fall a few short of the majority, the estimates for the South are probably too conservative. In 1942, a very close election, the South and the Border gave 129 seats to the Democrats. Moreover, in 1944 there were 9 congressmen chosen in at-large elections. Party advantages would depend upon the states in which those elections occurred. In 1944 the Democrats won six and the Republicans three.

This normal sectional pattern will not necessarily continue, if there is any large-scale reorganization of the American party system. Fifteen years ago there were persons who looked for a geographic particularization of the party system, but it did not materialize. At present there are strong evidences that the Democratic liberal party may not for long be able to maintain its official integrity in the face of the decided contradictions which exist within its fold. If the conservative Southern Democratic congressmen continue to battle against policies which are "musts" with liberal Democratic leaders from the other sections, the Roosevelt party may well disintegrate. Thereafter, we would find ourselves with three strong parties, each of which would be sectional in its strength. Under such conditions, our national administration would inevitably become a coalition of at least two parties.

Index

Agrarian party system: 20
Agrarianism: decline of, 12; development in West, 14
Amendment: Seventeenth, 5; Nineteenth, 30
American Labor party: 27, 84
American Socialist Labor party: 22
Apportionments of House of Representatives: 6–8
Artificial Decade: *vii*
At-large elections: 51

Border: defined, 9n.; representation of, 10, 11; party strength in, 86–88
Bryan, William Jennings: 20, 32, 37, 41

Calhoun, John C.; 15, 18
Candidacies, number in study: 51
Cannon, Joe: 25
Civil War, end of an era: 14
Clash of parties: 56
Cleveland, Grover: 20, 23
Commons, British House of, size: 8
Composite picture of party strength: 96–101
Congress: loss of popular esteem, *vii;* "rubber stamp", *viii;* primary organ of democracy, 3; little power added to, 4; specific powers of, 4; Seventy First, 25; may suffer from decrease in off-year vote, 35–36; coalition nature of, 40; political stalemate in, 40
Congressional districts: importance of, 50, 51

Congressional elections: 1920, 23; 1930, 23n.; 1936, 23; 1912, 24; 1914, 24; 1916, 24; 1918, 25; vote in presidential years, 35 ff.; vote in off years, 35 ff.
Coolidge, Calvin: *vii*

Democracy: American, 5; parliamentary, 28; based on individual, 32
Democratic party: victories, 34; revolt in, 41; "bad for business", 48; generality of strength, 60
Distribution of party strength: 58–61
District system: sectionalism, 79; in East, 80–86; in Border, 86–88; in South, 88–92; in Middle West, 92–95; in West, 95, 96
Douglas, Stephen A.: 17

East, defined, 9; record in representation, 11; normal party distribution, 85; and party records in, 80–86

Farmer-Labor party: 27, 76
Flynn, J. T.: 4n.
Foliart, James: *ix*
Freight-rate differentials, in South: 13
Fusion candidacies: *ix*
Fusionists: 27

Geography on side of freedom: 16
Grady, Henry: 12

Hamilton, Alexander: 5
Harding, Warren G.: *vii*
Hayek, Friedrich: 4n.
Holland, S. C.: *x*
Hoover, Herbert: *vii*, 42, 43
House of Representatives: size of, 5–8; size of apportionment quotas, 7–9; party membership in, 1896–1944, 27

Ideological parties: 65
Immigration, little in South: 12n.
Industrialism, rise of: 20–22

Industry in South: 12
Isms, emergence of: 14

Jay, John: 6
Jefferson, Thomas: 5, 15, 29

LaFollette, R. M., Sr.: 62–64
Laissez-faire liberalism: 21
Legislative bodies, loss of faith in by electorate: 38
Legislature, proper size of: 9
Liberty, traditional human: 5
Local party organization: toughness of, 39; importance of, 40
Lowering voting age, reasons for: 31

Majority control, party successful in presidential elections: 24–26
Majority vote, number of seats won by: 52–56
Marshall, Thomas: 63, 64
Middle West: defined, 9n.; role of, 13; party strength in, 92–95
Mill, John Stuart: 18
Minorities, natural: 10
Missouri Compromise: 16
Monroney, A. S. (Mike): *v*
Mugwumps: 23
Muckrakers: 21
McClure's Magazine: 21
McKinley, William: 37

National Political Action Committee: 36n.
Negroes: methods of barring from voting in South, 32–33; political strength in sections other than South, 39
New Deal: *viii*
Norris, George: 25, 42

Obscurantism: 32
Oden, William: *ix*
Opportunism in politics: *ix*

Paine, Thomas: 15

Parker, A. B.: 41
Parliament, British, "Mother of Parliaments": 3
Party politics, beginning of: 20
Party program, violations of: 49, 50
Party strength: percentage categories, 58–61; composite picture, 96–101
Party success, 1896–1944: 23
Party system: institutionalism of, 51; function of, 90; in Middle West, 92–95; in West, 95, 96
Party ticket, popularity of: 43–45
Plurality system: evaluation of, 83; in Border, 86–88; in South, 88–92; in Middle West, 92–95; in West, 95, 96
Political campaigns, characteristics of: 28–29
Popular vote totals by years and parties: 33
Populist party: 27, 37
Presidential candidates, popularity of: 43–45
Presidential Elections: 9n., 30n.
Pressure groups: vii
Progressive party: 25, 27; of 1912, 62; of 1924, 62, 63

Quinlan, Wayne: ix

Reason: Age of, 15; and slavery, 15
Reed, Thomas: 23
Representation loss by agrarian states: 12
Republican candidates, number of: 52
Republican party: revolt in, 41, 42; victories, 34; nothing to gain in South, 39; consistency of strength, 46–48
Revolt of 1910: 25
Reynolds, Quintelle: x
Roman legislative institutions: 3
Roosevelt, Franklin D.: 24, 32, 34, 35; coalition of, 54
Russell, Charles E.: 21

Scott, Travis: x
Sectional representation: 19

Sectionalism: aspects of American politics, 9; in party strength, 101–104

Slavery lost the battle in Washington: 17

Slaves: Negro, not counted fully in representation, 10; total, 10; increase in, 11; cost of Civil War, 14, 15

Smith, Adam: *vii*

South: defined, 9n.; decline in political importance, 10–13; export of population, 12; raw materials of, 12, 13; lag in voting, 32; vote in election of 1896, 32–34; vote in 1928, 32; whites disfranchised, 33–34; unavailability of candidates from, 39; revolts of its congressmen, 39; normal party strength, 88–92; non-Democratic strength in, 90–92

Social Democratic movement first appears in American politics: 21

Socialists: 65

Socialist Labor party: 65

Splinter parties: 50

States, admission of new: 7, 8

Steffens, Lincoln: 21

Straight-ticket voting: 37

Supreme Court Judges 1789–1937: 9n.

Tarbell, Ida: 21

Taft, William Howard, desertion of: 42

Third parties: 26, 27; wholesome function of, 65–66; candidates, 67, 74; dimunition in popularity of, 68; and the New Deal, 69; earlier ones, 70; sectional character of, 71–72; congressmen elected, 72; control of election winners, 73–74; strength in West, 75; in East and Middle West, 75, 76; in South, 76; in Border, 77

Third-term tradition: 24

Three-fifths' clause: 10

Tilden, Samuel J.: 20

TVA: 12

Tyranny: 4

Vote totals: in twenty-five elections, 30; increase due to women's suffrage, 30; immigration, 31; natural increase, 31; lengthening of life by medical science, 31; national psychology, 31; literacy, 31–32; increase by sections of 1928 and 1944 over 1896, 33 n., 34
Virginia representation: 7

Wallace, Henry: 39
War, effect of on voting: 35
West: defined, 9 n.; evolution of, 14; normal party strength of, 95, 96
Wilson, Woodrow: 40, 47
Women's suffrage: effect of in West, Middle West, and South, 30; percentage it increased 1920 vote over 1916, 30 n.

Yancey: 18

Congressional Elections

HAS BEEN SET

IN THE TEN POINT SIZE OF

LINOTYPE JANSON

AND PRINTED UPON

WOVE ANTIQUE

PAPER

UNIVERSITY OF OKLAHOMA PRESS

NORMAN